TEACHER, THE CHILDREN ARE HERE
A GUIDE FOR TEACHERS OF THE ELEMENTARY GRADES

Dianne Appleman

Johanna McClear

Scott, Foresman and Company
Glenview, Illinois   London

To Herb
For being with us every step of the way

372.11
Ap 5x
146226
mar.1989

Good Year Books
are available for preschool through grade 12 and for
every basic curriculum subject plus many enrichment
areas. For more Good Year Books, contact your local
bookseller or educational dealer. For a complete
catalog with information about other Good Year
Books, please write:
Good Year Books
Department GYB
1900 East Lake Avenue
Glenview, Illinois 60025

2 3 4 5 6 BKC 93 92 91 90 89 88

ISBN 0-673-38001-7

Page ix, excerpt from Natalie Babbitt's speech at the
Every Child Children's Book Conference, August,
1985. Used by permission of Natalie Babbitt.

Page 70, from *Chicago Poems* by Carl Sandburg,
copyright 1916 by Holt, Rinehart and Winston, Inc.;
renewed 1944 by Carl Sandburg. Reprinted by
permission of Harcourt Brace Jovanovich, Inc.

Contents

ACKNOWLEDGMENTS

Many colleagues, educators, parents, and friends read *Teacher, The Children Are Here* in manuscript, encouraged our work, and offered suggestions for revisions. Our book is better for their help.

In particular, we'd like to thank Ellen Adderley, Marc Appleman, Grant Brown, Margaret Burch, Barbara Castellana, Carol Clark, Roberta Columbus, Ronald Columbus, Jan Connor, Walt Connor, Sharon Cooper, John Denio, Suzanne Denio, Adriane de Windt, Lois Dreyer, Natalie Elman, Wendy Geoghegan, Harriet Griffith, Alice Hart, Carol Hyatt, Kathryn Nickum, John Nickum, Kaye Paauw, Joan Read, Thomas Read, Linda Shapiro, Judy Trunsky, Eve Van Rennes, Cecilia Vettraino, and Ellen Woodfin.

We also want to thank the Librarians in the Children's Room of the Bloomfield Township Library in Bloomfield Hills, Michigan: Barbara Klein, Caroline Nagengast, Marian Rafal, and Diana Vollmayer.

Most of all, we want to thank Herbert Appleman, to whom this book is dedicated.

Finally, we are grateful to Arnold Cheyney and Randy Steinheimer for their thoughtful reviews of the manuscript.

Preface

Photograph by Jack Kausch / Courtesy of Cranbrook, Educational Community

TO TEACH YOU OUR EXPERIENCE

A father asked his three-year-old daughter, "What's new?" The child answered, "Everything." Right now, as a first-year teacher, you probably feel very much like that child. That's why we've written *Teacher, The Children Are Here*. It's our attempt to teach you our experience, to walk you through your first year of teaching, beginning in August before the children arrive, and ending the following August, as you get ready for your second year in the classroom.

To write this book, we met once or twice a week and often on weekends, over a period of two years. Our workplace was a table in the children's section of our neighborhood library. (We chose the children's section because no one there pointed a finger and said "Shush"!)

We talked and made notes and had a wonderful time remembering the early days of our teaching careers—how we'd changed and the things we'd learned along the way. In retrospect, we laughed a lot.

Always, as we wrote and rewrote the several drafts of this book, we tried to put ourselves in your shoes and to answer the questions we thought you'd find most pressing. In addition, we tried to alert you to other questions you might not be aware of yet but that we knew from experience were lying in wait for you.

Incidentally, this experience adds up to a combined total of over fifty years of parenting and nearly forty years of teaching in public schools and independent schools. However, it's only fair to say that for the last ten years we've been colleagues in an independent school, located in a suburb of Detroit, and most of our material is drawn from this context.

We hope, however, that you'll see beyond the specifics, which may not apply to your situation, and focus on the general principles, which should be of value to any teacher. In this regard, we've been heartened by the example of Sylvia Ashton Warner's memoir, *Teacher*; although it's about Maori children in a small school in New Zealand, it's been a source of delight and instruction to teachers in all kinds of schools throughout the world.

As you read this book, you'll soon realize that we didn't confine ourselves to topics of information, such as lesson plans, because teaching is more than having technical skills and knowing subject matter; teaching is also the art of working with children, parents, and colleagues, of getting to understand them, empathize with them, help them, and—if you're very good and they're very receptive—inspire them. Accordingly, there are many chapters that deal with the psychological and emotional dimensions of teaching, such as being sensitive to gender differences, handling discipline problems, and developing good relationships with parents.

Inevitably, we've been forced to refer to "the child," as if this one word accurately described the hundreds of different children we've taught and that you'll come to teach. Of course, there's no such creature. As Natalie Babbitt, the author of *Tuck Everlasting*, noted with insight and delicious humor, "The Child," as idealized in capital letters and quotation marks, is a convenient fiction. You can tell because

"THE CHILD," once out of diapers, does not cry.

"THE CHILD" is beautiful and honest and never without a Kleenex.

"THE CHILD" watches some television, but accepts parental guidance cheerfully and would rather read anyway.

"THE CHILD" is clean all the time, except when being picturesquely dirty.

"THE CHILD" is never sick, except for measles, mumps and chicken pox, which are passed through with forebearance, dispatch and without scratching.

"THE CHILD" is not afraid of swimming or the dark or dogs or great Aunt Hepsibah's moustache.

"THE CHILD" has better manners than Amy Vanderbilt.

"THE CHILD" will qualify for Harvard without ever being a bookworm or a grind.

"THE CHILD" in short, will go out into the world and stun everyone, especially jealous relatives, with his or her splendid genetic make-up and obviously superior parenting—a combination of nature and nurture impossible to improve on, thereby insuring lasting self-satisfaction for "The Parent."

"THE CHILD" then, is . . . utterly different from anyone we know personally.

To ensure that we didn't saddle you with this nonexistent "CHILD," we've included, where appropriate, as many anecdotes about particular children as we remembered, and we've interspersed, between chapters, selections from the Memory Books of second-graders we've taught.

In our classes, Memory Books are written at the end of the year to give the children a chance to look back and to provide them with a souvenir album of their classmates. If these selections tend to be neater and have better spelling than you might expect, it's because the books are meant to be kept; consequently, the children are encouraged to revise their selections, with help from the teacher.

We hope that these anecdotes and memories will give a vivid sense of school life, of real students in real situations, and will remind you that children are often a source of fun and wonder, and that teaching is often an experience of humor and joy.

Nevertheless, we were concerned that such a large number of anecdotes might undermine our serious intentions. Fortunately, we came across a statement in *The Healing Heart*, by Norman Cousins, that dispelled our doubts:

*T**he writer makes his living by anecdotes. He searches them out and craves them as the raw materials of his profession. No hunter stalking his prey is more alert to the presence of his quarry than a writer looking for small incidents that cast a strong light on human behavior. If nothing is valid to the scientist except as it proceeds from masses of data, very little has meaning to the writer except as it is tied to the reality of a single person.*

You may not agree with everything we say or the strategies we recommend. That's all right. Our hope is that you'll treat this book as an information file, a suggestive guide, and an experienced friend who wants to be helpful.

You're probably thinking that these fine words are all well and good, but right now I'm facing an emergency: How in the world am I going to think up enough things for those kids to do between 8:00 A.M. and 3:00 P.M.?

Take heart, we promise you that one day you and the children will suddenly look up, shake your heads, smile, and say, "Is it three o'clock already?"

EVERYONE GETS BUTTERFLIES

Beginnings are exciting and challenging, and yet for many of us they can be very scary. We often feel inadequate and vulnerable at the beginning of a new experience. Children confide that they don't sleep very well before the first day of school. Neither do most teachers, and this is the first common bond between student and teacher.

I Was Really Worried

I was really worried the night before school began. My mother wanted me to wear a dress. But I wanted to wear my new pink jeans and the polo shirt that had flowers on it. We had a fight and I cried. She let me wear the jeans!

I was worried that the books would be too hard. My best friend, Jill, was in the other class. I was worried that I wouldn't have any friends.

I was worried about a lot of things.

by Paula

1
Before the First Week
of Class

Photograph by Taro Yamasaki/Courtesy of Cranbrook Educational Community

SETTING UP YOUR CLASSROOM

Alone in Your Room

A week or so before school begins, sit down in the middle of your classroom, all alone. Visualize the children who will share this room with you for the next ten months. Listen for the hum, and imagine the way you want your class to be: a community, almost a second home, where children can feel secure, learn academic skills and, more important, learn to learn and to share.

Consider the tools you think students will need for this adventure and plan an ordered environment, free from distractions—one that will stimulate clear thinking and provide plenty of room for energetic activity.

After a while, even though you have no particular plan in mind, you'll find yourself looking into cupboards, unpacking boxes, and thumbing through workbooks. As you relax and get to feel at home, you'll begin to think about the overall arrangement of your room.

Room Arrangement for the Beginning of School

Prepare a work/study area for each child so that his or her desk faces toward the chalkboard and the teacher's desk and away from exterior distractions such as doors to busy hallways or windows that open out to the playground. Be sure to use natural and artificial light to best advantage. For example, children should always face away from direct sunlight.

In addition to desks, you'll want other pieces of furniture in the room. Decide on which pieces you want, measure the space available, and then begin scavenging. Where? In your attic, at the Salvation Army, in a friend's basement, at a garage sale. Be ingenious! Keep an eye out for a soft chair for yourself, an adult-size rocking chair, a child-size rocking chair, round tables for group work, a table for the math center so that you can keep projects on exhibit for several days, screens or furniture to separate areas, beanbags for children to cuddle up in while they're reading, pillows, a throw rug, bins for math materials, and storage for art materials.

These additions will give the room a warm, informal, cozy atmosphere. You may not want to have them in the room immediately, because they invite informality, and the class, at this point, may require more structure. Plan to introduce them gradually.

*E*ven though it was only the beginning of the year, the children had already fallen in love with certain books, especially Where The Wild Things Are *and its mischievous hero, Max.*

I decided to encourage this love of reading by creating a cozy, comfortable reading corner, complete with pillows. I brought four or five soft pillows from home.

As I drove to school, I imagined several children curled up with pillows, reading away. Instead, when they saw the pillows, the children became the wild beasts of the story and began tossing the pillows back and forth at each other. Disappointed, I put the pillows away.

Later in the year one of the children found the pillows, took them out, spread himself comfortably on the carpet, and began reading a book. It was just as if, several months later, in his own good time, Max had tamed the wild beast!

Now that you have the furniture in place, at least for the moment, and a vision of how the room may be transformed in the coming months, it's time to consider what materials you and the children will be using and where those materials will be stored.

Locations for Basic Materials

First, designate one permanent storage place for teacher materials such as

Lesson plan book

Grading book

Folder for a substitute teacher containing class list, seating chart, daily plan, names of children with special needs

Box with written communications from school to be sent to parents

Personal calendar

Personal favorite stories and books to be read to the entire class

Games to be played with the entire class

Ditto sheets

School handbook

Files with magazine and newspaper articles

Reference books (dictionary and thesaurus)

Curriculum manuals

Teachers' editions of textbooks

*M*aria was very curious about my teacher's edition of our reader. So, because she was a precocious student, I let her borrow the book and asked her to prepare the next day's lesson on fairy tales.

I'll never forget the lesson she conducted.

"Don't argue with me. I have the answers in this book . . ."

"Write an essay on 'Rumpelstiltskin.' You have exactly ten seconds!"

I was very grateful to Maria; she made me seem like an angel of mercy.

Then, designate permanent storage places for children's materials:

A rack for scissors

A shelf for jars of paste

Trays for paper

Containers for crayons

Pegboard for earphones

Boxes for completed work

Boxes for work not yet completed

A box for each child (similar to a mailbox), where completed work to be taken home is placed

A teacher can also use a child's mailbox to send him a personal message.
Since everyone loves to get mail, this is an excellent way to sneak in a reading lesson.
Mr. White, our first-grade teacher, wrote such delightful letters that children saved them for years.
I remember one, in particular, because it was sent to my neighbor's son.

"Dear Jeremy,
If you happen to be missing a left-handed glove, you might want to look on the fourth step of the staircase near the art room.

Your friend,

Sherlock Holmes"

Now that you've arranged the furniture and organized the materials and books so that you and the children will be able to find things and keep the room fairly well ordered, your next job is to make sure that the first impression of the room will be an inviting one. The best way to do this is by creating interesting and attractive bulletin boards.

Bulletin Boards for Outside the Room

Plan a bulletin board for the first day that will include all the children's names. This will serve many purposes:

Each child will feel important if his name is up somewhere in the room.

Each child likes the chance to look for his own name.

The children get to know each other's names.

Each child will see himself as part of the group (this is a feeling that you want to encourage from the very beginning).

You can put this bulletin board on a wall outside the room. A simple and popular design is a large arrow of bright, primary colors. The arrow points toward the room and each child's name is part of the arrow.

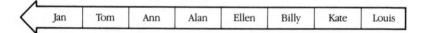

| Jan | Tom | Ann | Alan | Ellen | Billy | Kate | Louis |

(If you don't feel you are creative in this way, don't worry, there are books you can consult to give you ideas.)

Bulletin Boards for Inside the Room

When the children come in on the first day of school, the room should be bright, interesting, and give a promise of wonderful things to come.

It's also important to give the room a feeling of harmony. A good way to do this is by coordinating colors. If you use colors to relate A to B, and C to D, the children will find the room less confusing. For example, you might use light blue as a background for the bulletin boards, yellow plastic bins to hold the math materials, and yellow-and-blue plaid contact paper to cover the art tables.

Another way to gain harmony is by setting up display areas according to subject. This means that you'll have to decide on different spots for language arts, a calendar, and art work. These spots should correspond to your learning centers. When display and center areas stay in the same spot throughout the year, the children know what to expect, and you eliminate extra work and planning.

Three Basic Bulletin Boards

Cover a bulletin board with bright background paper. By the end of the first day, display a piece of each child's work on this board at children's eye level. It makes the children feel very proud and provides an incentive for them to return the next day. Often, a young child will bring a parent into the room to show what she's already accomplished.

Another bulletin board that we love to put up highlights information and pictures about the fall season and suggests weekend outings for the children and their families. Since our school is in southeastern Michigan, this bulletin board notes cider mills in the area, schedules of college football games, and road routes to observe the autumn colors and the migration of the monarch butterflies (which fly from northern Canada to Point Pelee, where they stop for a brief rest before taking off for their ultimate destination in California and Mexico). It's convenient if this bulletin board lends itself to frequent changes. For example, a tree can have colored leaves in September, bare branches in November, and snowflakes in December.

Finally, prepare a "Helper" bulletin board, designating enough jobs so that everyone in the class has something meaningful to do. If there are twenty children, think of twenty jobs, such as getting the snack, taking attendance, and cleaning the guinea pig cage. Again, it's convenient if you design this chart so that names rotate to new jobs each week. For example, take a piece of white card-

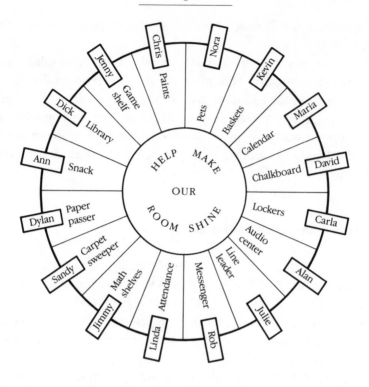

board and cut out a circle, approximately 20 inches in diameter. In the center of the circle, paste a yellow sun. Around the sun, paste a number of rays of two alternating colors. On each ray write the name of a job that has to be done in your classroom. Then attach a clothespin, with a different child's name on it, to each ray. At the beginning of the next week, rotate the clothespins so that each child is assigned to a new job.

GETTING TO KNOW YOUR SCHOOL

Read the School Handbook

If the school handbook or any printed materials are available, read them; then you won't be surprised by school regulations or traditions.

Scooter the Guinea Pig

My best memory was the first day we got Scooter. I didn't even notice Scooter in his cage near the books. Susannah was picked first to clean his cage for the first two weeks. Then some other people were picked to clean his cage for the next two weeks. At last, my turn came Everybody in the room got a chance to clean his cage. Scooter is a super guinea pig.

By Pritham

I *can remember arriving in the dining room for lunch on the first day in my new school. I didn't know that you were supposed to stand behind your chair until a signal was given for everyone to be seated. As a result, 75 children and teachers were standing and one person was sitting. Guess who?*

Read the School Syllabus

If the curriculum is prescribed and available in a syllabus, take time during the summer to read, think about, and absorb the material. If choices about curriculum are left up to the individual teacher, make your choices over the summer and provide a framework or outline that will be in place before you arrive at school for the first all-staff meeting. Once school begins, there will be less time to devote to this important step.

Focus on all courses of study, including subjects such as play, athletics, dramatics, music, art and the homeroom program.

Acquaint Yourself with the Layout of the School Building

Locate rooms, offices, and areas such as

Art room

Music room

Science room

Library

Reading resource room

Speech therapist's office

Nurse's office

Supply rooms

Copy services area: xeroxing, mimeographing, laminating

Lunchroom

Gymnasium

Playground

Explore the nooks and crannies and surrounding grounds so that when school begins, you'll know at least as much as the children do and not feel like a stranger.

Hand in your order early for supplies that are in demand.

I wish I'd known to check out the art supply closet the first week I started teaching. By the second week, every piece of red paper was gone.

Why? Because Christmas and Valentine's Day were coming up and the old timers, thinking ahead, had raided the joint!

Visit the School Library

Ask the librarian to go through the section that's appropriate for your class, and to let you know what magazines, films, filmstrips, cassettes, computer software, and media catalogues are available. (For an annotated list of magazines that children enjoy, see Appendix B.)

Then arrange for a time when she can instruct you in the use of the audio/visual equipment. Such equipment seems to vary from school to school and from year to year. There's nothing worse than that moment when you have the class poised to learn from an audio/visual experience and you can't get the movie projector to work.

Ask about the ways the librarian helps the classroom teacher. Does she read stories to the children, introducing them to new books, authors, and illustrators?

Does she give instruction in library skills (how to look up authors, titles and subjects in the card catalogue; how to find books on the shelves using the call numbers)?

Does she help the children do research for a report, using reference materials and books? (For example, if the student is assigned a paper on the culture of ancient Egypt, does she guide him to the shelves and the encyclopedias? Does she help him use the card catalogue by pointing out subject headings, such as *pyramid* and *hieroglyphic?*)

Does she run a Young Author's Program where children write, edit, illustrate, and actually construct their own books? (In such programs, the children read each other's books and vote for their favorites; the books selected by the children are then entered in a local author's fair, usually sponsored by a university.)

It's wise to work closely with the librarian. In addition to the aforementioned services, she can acquaint you with new books to enrich your curriculum, since she reads reviews in *Booklist, Horn Book, Kirkus,* and *Library Journal.*

Finally, it's a good idea to discuss with her the books that your students are choosing to take out of the library. Every year some child will take home a book that is much too advanced for her. Inevitably an irritated parent will call to complain.

I know my daughter has read and enjoyed Judy Blume books since second grade, but she shouldn't have been given Are You There God? It's Me, Margaret. *Although my daughter's in fourth grade now, there's material in this book that confused her. In case you don't know, it describes a girl getting her period!*

Meet with the Secretary, the Custodian, and the Kitchen Staff

The Secretary
Ask the secretary to describe her role and what she expects from you. A secretary can be very helpful. Often a warm and caring

relationship will develop that will make her office a pleasant oasis for you. So drop by, say hello, and prepare to be impressed as you find out how much she does. For example, her duties usually include:

Sorting and distributing mail

Recording attendance and late arrivals

Distributing handouts for children to take home

Arranging for accident or emergency care when the school nurse is unavailable

Taking homework requests from parents for children who are ill

Preparing permission slips for trips

Arranging transportation for trips

Keeping on file school supply catalogues

Serving as the lost-and-found center

Reimbursing expenses

Informing teachers about available monies

Forwarding phone messages (The few times each year that my husband phoned me at school, the secretary realized that these were important calls and offered to take over my class so that I could speak to him in private. This courtesy was appreciated beyond words.)

The Custodian

The custodian can be a good friend to you and the class. Know where and how to reach him in case of an emergency. Ask him what the class can do, at the end of the day, to make his after-school cleaning easier. For example, he'll probably want the children to put up their chairs on scheduled vacuuming days.

The Kitchen Staff

If your school provides food services,

find out exactly what they are: meals, snacks, parties?

find out how to get materials for cooking projects without disturbing the kitchen routine.

Meet with Specialists Who Support Classroom Teachers

The Reading Specialist

Learn when the reading specialist is available for consultation, testing, diagnosis, and working with children. Look over the resources in her room. Ask her to recommend supplementary materials for children who are learning English as a second language. Find out whether there are special activity sheets that go along with the school's basal reading series. Discuss tests and procedures used by the school to assess reading skills. Finally, set times for small-group remediation and for individual students who'll need her most.

*R*eading is a subject that looms large in a first-grader's mind.
Cindy stood at the door of my classroom, refusing to come in.
I asked her what the matter was.
"I can't ... read."
"I'll teach you."
"It's too hard."
"I assure you, in a few months, you'll be reading."
But obviously, Cindy wasn't reassured, because her eyes became teary.
I didn't know what to say next when, suddenly, I remembered that she had a brother in second grade.
"Your brother learned, didn't he?"
Cindy began to smile.
If he could learn, anyone could.
A minute later, she walked into the room.

The Speech Therapist
Ask the speech therapist about time available for consultation, testing, and diagnosis. Ask about special instruction for children with speech problems.

*A*nd as the year goes on, don't be surprised at the things you hear outside the speech therapist's office.
 One day, passing by, I overheard the following conversation between two third-graders.
 "What did you work on in speech today?"
 "I practiced saying brefist."

The School Psychologist
Ask the psychologist about situations that you should be aware of concerning children with learning problems (Is a child unable to concentrate?), emotional problems (Does a child have difficulty leaving home to come to school?), and family problems (Is there a divorce pending?).

Find out when he's available for consultation, working with teachers, seeing students, and meeting with parents.

The School Nurse
Check the nurse's schedule—know when she's in the building and whom to contact if she's unavailable. Discuss emergency accident procedures. Ask about accident forms—where they are and how they should be filled out. Find out when a child should be sent home because of illness. (It's usually appropriate to send him home if he has a fever.)

Ask about the preferred way to communicate with parents in case of minor or long-term illness. (Should the contact be between teacher and parent or between nurse and parent? During school hours or in the evening?)

Finally, discuss ongoing health education. (Do girls and boys meet separately with the nurse to talk about male and female changes in the body? Are there classes in substance abuse and what it means and how it affects a child's life?)

The Academic Specialists

Ask about the programs taught by the science teacher, music teachers (vocal, instrumental, strings), art teacher, and physical education teacher.

The science teacher can tell you what units he covers in your grade and when they'll be taught. This will help you to coordinate some of your classroom ideas with his. He'll tell you whether he plans to take the children on field trips and how you can prepare the children for each trip.

The music teachers will let you know whether your class will be involved in a production or whether they want you to work on reviewing words to songs in the classroom.

The art teacher may work on projects in conjunction with a social studies unit. For example, for a unit on Alaska, the art teacher may have the class paint a mural showing a snow scene with polar bears, seals, walruses, and caribou.

The physical education teacher may alert you to problems of physical coordination that are getting in the way of learning in the classroom.

Get to Know Your Community

Every community has a history, with landmarks and places of interest that have been preserved. The local library usually has paintings and photographs that reveal how the community has changed over the years, and there may even be pamphlets or books that tell your community's story in detail. Acquaint yourself with these places and materials so that you can bring them to the attention of your class during the year. It's important for children to know about the community they live in and how it came to be the way it is.

More specifically, find out about any educational programs that are available in your area. For example, the Science Institute in our city offers ongoing programs in nature studies (a honey harvest, a maple sugar harvest, and a fall, winter, and spring walk to observe the changing landscape). These events are likely to be

---

popular with the schools in your area, which means that now, in September, there are probably few, if any, visiting times left. (Remember to schedule your appointments for the coming year as the spring term winds down in June.)

Explore other facilities in your community: museums, libraries, athletic fields, nature centers, and educational institutions.

Meet with Your Teaching Partner

Plan to go out to lunch so that your meeting with your teaching partner can be personal, leisurely, and uninterrupted. In your discussion over lunch:

Coordinate your daily schedule; that is, plan for recess time together, for a storytime that includes both classes, and for a coffee break (when both classes are with other teachers) so that you can meet to plan or maybe just to talk.

Ask about schedules for special subjects. How often does the class go to science, music, art, and physical education?

Ask about your lunchtime responsibilities. (Are you supposed to teach table manners and encourage interesting conversation?)

Review procedures for recess. (What are the school safety rules? Do all children use all equipment? Do children stay indoors if they have a minor illness? If so, where do they stay, and who's responsible for them? Can you keep children in from recess to complete homework or because of poor behavior?)

Review procedures for fire drills. (How do you leave the building from your classroom? If your class is with another teacher, who's responsible?)

Review procedures for weather emergencies. (How will you be informed if the school is to be closed because of a snowstorm? If the children are sent home during the school day because weather conditions are growing worse, what happens to the child whose parents can't be reached?)

Review procedures for dismissal. (What happens if a child is not picked up?)

Plan to coordinate room parties and field trips. (Will both classes celebrate children's birthdays together? Will you have holiday parties together? How much will parents be involved in the plans for these parties?)

In addition, ask questions about:

Parent events (Are teachers responsible for attending a Sunday afternoon Ice Cream Social sponsored by the parents?)

Conference scheduling (Do you call the parents for an appointment or does the school secretary?)

Bulletin boards (Are you responsible for bulletin boards other than those in your own classroom?)

During this first meeting, be a good listener. Offer your ideas for discussion; don't announce them as edicts. Give your partner breathing room; don't come on too strong or expect to establish a deep friendship in forty minutes. Be sensitive to the ways in which your partner's interests and personality are different from yours; be willing to appreciate these differences.

Meet with the Head of Your School

You've already explored many aspects of the school. Now you have only a few well-chosen policy questions to ask. This is the perfect time to get to know your "boss" better. The start of the school year is a busy time for him, too, so make your appointment early. Don't be surprised, however, if he can't see you immediately, and don't take it personally if he cancels at the last minute. Be patient. When you do meet him, discuss such questions as

Are all teachers in a grade expected to teach the same things at the same time? How much individuality is encouraged within each class?

What is the purpose of a homework assignment? How much time is a child expected to devote to homework? Is it considered appropriate for parents to help children with homework assignments?

What are the guidelines for written communication with the home?

What are the expectations for school discipline? For classroom discipline?

What reporting and grading system is used? Is it different in different grades? How? Why? What are the guidelines for evaluation of students?

Is it helpful or appropriate to be informed of the school's admissions policy?

How are teachers evaluated?

How may a teacher benefit from available perks such as funds for further education, sabbaticals, or leaves of absence?

PLANNING FOR THE FIRST WEEK OF SCHOOL

Study Your Class List

One year I was supposed to have 24 students in my class. But on the first day of school, 31 students marched into my room. I couldn't believe it. I was sure some of them belonged elsewhere.

One boy, who looked particularly lost, confirmed my suspicion.

"What room is this?" he asked.
"214," I said.
"What's your name?"
"Mrs. Damon."
There was a long pause.
"What school *is this?"*

Study Each Child's Records

Learn the children's names and, if possible, consider their name preferences and nicknames.

Then list the children by birth dates to find out who is the youngest, the oldest, and who has repeated a grade and when.

Next, read each child's permanent file and note any important information that will help you this first week. But don't prejudge the child; make an effort to see him as he is *now*. Remember George Bernard Shaw's line about his tailor: "He was the wisest of men. Every time I met him, he took my measure anew."

If problems are noted, speak to last year's teachers.

Finally, make a notebook with a page for each child. Jot down important information such as

Birth date

The child's position in the family

The age and sex of each sibling

Any information about the family such as adoption or divorce

The telephone number where the child's parents can be reached in case of emergency

Health information such as previous illnesses

Allergies

Food dislikes

Previous schooling (and the child's feelings about the experience)

Be on the lookout for other information that might be of help, such as different last names that indicate remarriage, the recent arrival of a baby in the family, siblings or relatives in the school, the home language of the child if it isn't English, unusual travel experiences, and the parents' occupations. By having this information you'll get to know the child, and the child will realize you care and be grateful for your concern.

New Students

Note new students. In the first few days of the school year, they'll require special attention and an extra measure of support. Plan to make yourself available to them in unstructured situations such as recess, lunchtime, and dismissal.

Separation Problems

Children, especially in the primary grades, may have difficulty separating from their parents at the beginning of school. You'll have to be sympathetic of course. But sympathy won't be enough; you'll have to be ingenious, too.

*B*obby was a tall, sturdy first-grader. Each day he arrived at school happy, and separated easily from his mother. However, about mid-morning Bobby would break into tears. Nothing would comfort him—not a hug, not a snack, not a game. He just wanted his mom.

His parents and I agreed to try a "Call Home" plan. Whenever Bobby got that awful need-to-see-his-mom feeling, he'd go across the hall, call her on the telephone, say "Hello," chat for a minute, and return to the classroom all smiles. Within a week, Bobby had settled into first grade, and no longer even thought of "Dial-a-Mom."

Sometimes it's the parent who has separation difficulties. A good way to handle this is to get the parent involved productively in another part of the school.

L isa arrived in first grade with enthusiasm, sparkle, a keen interest to learn, and a mother. Every day, Lisa's mother brought her to school, stayed in the room for an hour, stopped back during the day, and came early when it was time to pick up Lisa. Since the desks and chairs were too small for an adult, I placed a larger chair outside the classroom door and asked Lisa's mother to please wait there. Over coffee, I learned that Lisa's mother was a talented gardener. I asked her if she could do something about the gardens outside the classroom that desperately required weeding. Soon she began to spend the better part of her day caring for the garden area. As the year progressed, she devoted more and more time to beautifying all the gardens around the school.

Lisa is now a freshman in college. Her mother still gardens at the school, and the lovely flowers that she tended have been appreciated by students, teachers, parents, and visitors for many years.

LESSON PLANS

Flexibility is the key to planning lessons, especially in the beginning. Alternate lessons with games, songs, hands-on activities, and quiet times. (If the children have been sitting for 40 minutes in a music class, you'll want to have a more energetic activity ready for them when they return to you.) Be sure your lesson plans include not only academic subjects and games, but transitions, free-choice time, and recess.

Academic Subjects

Read a story to the group and discuss it afterward.

Have the children take turns reading aloud from a magazine, an article, or a story.

Read with individuals and begin individual assessments.

Have the children do a simple writing assignment. Take note of their vocabulary, spelling, and handwriting skills.

In math, give a problem orally; then observe how quickly the children figure out what operation is needed to solve it. Use Bingo or fact cards to see how quickly and accurately they add, subtract, multiply, and divide.

In art, set up individual, uncomplicated projects, such as making a collage. Assess their dexterity and creativity. (Do they make choices that surprise you? Are they bold in their use of shapes and colors?)

Games and Discussions

Play group games, such as Hangman, Geography, and Seven-Up to learn about the children's general knowledge and their ability to give and take in a group situation. Allow time for group discussions.

Transitions and Free-Choice Time

Talk to the children when they arrive in the morning, get ready to go on their way to lunch and recess, and when they get ready to go home. Observe them during transitions and unstructured activities. Note what they choose to do, how they organize their time, and how they interact.

Safety Awareness

During the first week, the children need to be made aware of the safety standards of the school and classroom. Teachers should periodically review these safety procedures, which include

Fire drill rules

Tornado or hurricane drill rules

Hallway rules

Lunchroom routines

Arrival and dismissal routines

Recess rules

Recess

Of course children must obey safety rules during recess. But apart from that, children should have an unstructured recess to give them some time of their own. They need the freedom to explore and stretch their boundaries.

You'll frequently run across the "volunteer" who elects to skip recess under the guise of being helpful or so terribly conscientious that she must complete *all* her spelling sentences. Such a student, who is apt to be ingenious and persistent, will go to great lengths to make you give in. Don't do it, and don't let her play your teaching partner against you. Actually, she's behaving this way because she has difficulty interacting with other children, or because the temperature has dropped below 60 degrees.

*M*rs. Adamson, our school nurse, always claimed that, although it was important to care for the children, it was just as important not to coddle them.
Unfortunately, Hilda, who was a big girl of ten, liked to be coddled.

*One day, coughing loudly and theatrically, she came
to Mrs. Adamson and announced, "I can't go out for
recess today. I think I have pneumonia."*

*Mrs. Adamson put her hand on Hilda's forehead. "Feels
normal to me."*

"But it's very cold out—"

*Mrs. Adamson nodded. "I know, dear. This is Michigan.
It's always cold in the winter. You have to get used to that.
If you don't you'll be stuck indoors from November
till May."*

*"But Mrs. Adamson, I'm coughing. Don't you
hear me?"*

*"Of course I hear you, sweetheart. You cough
very well."*

"Then don't you realize that—?"

*Mrs. Adamson was unmoveable. "I realize that you
should be outside playing. Either the cold air will make
you feel stronger and you'll get rid of your cough or—"*

"Or it'll give me pneumonia! And I'll—!"

"You'll prove that I was wrong."

Materials

Collect all the supplies, such as pencils, paper, and paints, that you think you'll need. Organize and label these materials clearly so that the children can use them on their own without directions from you.

Naturally, over the course of time, items will wear out and have to be replaced, but not, we hope, because they've been abused. In a room where materials are scattered about, broken, or have parts missing, you can be sure children are not learning and working to their maximum capacity.

Prepare teacher-made materials ahead of time. Don't worry if they aren't perfect. For your purpose, hand-made materials are often better than manufactured ones. The challenge of making your own materials is fun, creative, and encourages children to be resourceful and self-reliant.

Often, you can do this busy work at home while watching TV. Later on, parents may offer to assist you with some of these time-consuming tasks. Their assistance will be most welcome! Examples of items that can be prepared in advance are:

Individual dictionaries. Make a book for each child with the most commonly used words, leaving room on each page for the child to add his or her own entries.

Journals or diaries. Make a book of blank pages with a decorative cover, for recording daily or weekly experiences and impressions.

Softbooks. Make other books, of different sizes and shapes, for impromptu story writing.

Bulletin boards. Prepare art work and displays.

If appropriate, coordinate your thinking and planning with the other section or sections of your grade.

A Good Way to Frame the Week

Playing "Estimation" is a good way to frame the week. The game begins on Monday morning when you show the class a jar filled with pennies. Each child then writes down his estimate of how many pennies are in the jar, signs his name, and hands you the slip of paper.

The game ends on Friday afternoon when you turn over the jar, let the pennies spill out, and invite the children to count them. (An extra math lesson!) The child whose estimate is closest wins the prize.

As you can imagine, Friday afternoon is usually a tired time, when interest and energy are low. "Estimation" transforms it into the highlight of the week.

A final tip: to make each game different, choose different things to estimate. For example, on Monday morning you can have the boys' physical education teacher drop by the room. Then, after he's gone, you can ask the class to estimate his height to the nearest sixteenth of an inch. On Friday afternoon, when he returns, you can ask him to stand against the chalkboard and have someone measure his height with a yardstick. Or . . . No, we won't give any more suggestions. Half the fun is using your imagination!

Photograph by Taro Yamasaki/Courtesy of Cranbrook Educational Community

THE FIRST DAY OF SCHOOL

The Morning Begins: Helping Everyone Feel at Home

From the first introductions on the first day of school, the class is on its way to becoming a family. To make the students feel at home in this family, be sure to greet each child individually. A smile or a light touch on the shoulder will make him feel that you like him; a personal word about his name or clothing will make him feel that he's special.

After greeting the students, provide some time for them to explore the classroom and feel comfortable in it. Let them walk about, interact with other students, view various displays in the room, browse through books, and examine learning centers. While this is going on, spend a few moments with each child and be alert for signs of anxiety or separation sadness. It bears repeating that any child who has these feelings will require extra support in the first week and perhaps even in the coming weeks.

In addition to "Dial-A-Mom" and "Send Mom to the Garden," I can't help recalling another first-day drama.

One year, I spotted a very lonely, very sad little guy standing with one foot out the front door of the school building. The tears were pouring down his cheeks.

He was obviously looking for his mom or at the very least her car. I gently assisted him back into the building. As we were walking toward his classroom, he was able to control his crying long enough to say, "I was looking for my mommy because she misses me too much when I'm in school."

The First Activity: Making Introductions

To create a feeling of intimacy, gather the children together on the floor and introduce them to each other. Assign a special friend to each new child. Encourage the children to share some recent experiences with each other. Share some information about yourself, your family, your interests, or your pets, letting the age of the group dictate what you select to tell.

The Second Activity: Reading and Discussing an Article or Story

After the children begin to feel at ease, initiate a group discussion to motivate and set the stage for their first assignment. Suppose you're going to read an article about animal behavior. First ask about the children's experiences with animals. Then read the article together. During the reading you can make observations and mental notes about how they listen and pay attention. Often there are short-answer questions at the end of the story. Have the children read the questions aloud and guide their discussion. (Don't call on the children at this point since those with reading problems will be uncomfortable. Instead, ask for volunteers.)

The Third Activity: Writing Answers to Questions

If you feel that the children are ready and able, have them return to their seats and write the answers to the story questions. Meanwhile, stand back and observe how individuals approach their work. Note, for example, whether they

start to work right away.

drop their pencils.

get up to sharpen their pencils.

ask a friend for help.

Make yourself available to any children who are having difficulty. Store the information in your mind and, later in the day, find time to record it.

Be Sensitive to the Students' Attention Span

Until you know the children, you won't be able to predict the proper length of an activity. Since in the first few days you're weaning the children away from their carefree summer life, you may find that they have trouble sitting and concentrating. They may be able to work for 15 minutes, for 20 minutes, for 30 minutes. You'll have to be the judge.

The Fourth Activity: Doing Something Physical

As soon as the children become restless, move on to another activity. This should be a physical activity such as

A group game—Simple Simon

A group exercise—jumping jacks, touching toes, deep knee bends, jogging in place

An art activity—paper weaving or pastel drawing from life. Preface art activities with a demonstration and a discussion of work and clean-up procedures. After the children have completed the activity, have group sharing.

A Break in the Morning: Moving on to a Special Class

Now it's probably time for them to move on to a special class: drama, music, art, science, or physical education.

Before leaving the room, review the rules for walking in the hall: walk on the right-hand side of a hallway, speak in a soft voice, and keep up with the group.

If the teacher isn't ready to receive your children when you arrive at your destination, have some games in mind to keep them involved and orderly. Remember, before your colleagues get to know your true teaching abilities, they'll think you're a good teacher if your class is well-behaved!

The Fifth Activity: Introducing an Academic Subject

After the children return, you'll want to regroup for an academic activity such as math, reading, or social science. This may mean

independent work on math story problems. For those children who finish quickly, assign a bonus problem.

independent work on a pencil-and-paper task. Have each child complete a Story Starter and perhaps even illustrate his or her story.

independent work in a textbook. Plan and assign an activity that will be interesting yet easy enough so that the children will feel they are going to do well this year.

Be explicit when giving directions, encourage questions, and take time to clarify what you expect.

Another Break: Enjoying Snack Time

Now break for a snack (snacking is a favorite activity of all students). This is a good opportunity for quiet, one-to-one conversation. As with other activities, there should be procedures governing how the snack is distributed, where the children sit and, of course, clean-up.

After the children have had their snack, you'll want to provide time for a visit to the bathrooms. Since this is the first day of school, you may decide to walk the class there, to make sure they know exactly where the boys' and girls' rooms are.

When you get to the bathrooms, remind the children to use the facilities quickly and to wash their hands before coming out.

Then, to avoid chaos, send two boys in at a time and two girls in at a time.

The Sixth Activity: Writing Brief Autobiographies

After the children return to the room, ease them back into an academic routine by having them write or tell brief autobiographies. Have younger children write about parents, grandparents, brothers and sisters, a pet, or a personal experience such as riding a bike or playing in the leaves. (You may want to let very young children talk about their experiences before they start writing.)

Older children may write about seeing a play or a musical performance, going to a party, having a best or special friend, or pursuing a hobby.

If there's time before lunch, gather together to share these writings. This should be done on a voluntary basis, since some of the writings may be personal or youngsters may be shy early in the year. Collect the writings so that you can evaluate

language skills.

creative use of language.

grammar and punctuation.

personal likes, dislikes, and interests.

Just Before Lunch

Before breaking for lunch, review rules, procedures, and expectations to insure a smooth and pleasant experience.

Lunch and Recess

Teacher assignments for lunch and recess vary greatly from school to school. But it's safe to say that most schools will expect you to help out, at least once or twice a week, as a lunchroom or playground supervisor.

In those schools where teachers are scheduled to eat with the children, you'll also be expected to teach table manners and guide conversation.

A Moment to Relax

After lunch and recess, you'll want to let the children enjoy a quiet time of independent, free-choice reading of books and magazines in the class library. While they're reading, you can take a moment to relax, catch your breath, and mentally prepare for the afternoon.

A Break in the Afternoon: Moving on to Another Special Class

Now the children will probably be scheduled to go to another teacher's room for a special class. You can use this time to

have a cup of coffee.

communicate with a teaching partner, special teachers, or administrative personnel.

prepare for upcoming activities and lessons.

correct workbooks or papers.

attend to clerical or personal matters.

communicate with parents by telephone.

write letters to be sent home.

observe classes. (You may wish to accompany your children to a special class sometime within the first two weeks of school to observe them in another setting.)

The Seventh Activity: Reviewing the Day

After the children return, you'll want to regroup for a moment of sharing and reflecting. This is a good time to convey your excitement and enthusiasm for the coming year. Review the day. Talk about what happened and what has been accomplished.

*W*hen *a child goes home, a parent often says, "What did you do in school today? What did you learn?" Usually, the child says, "Nothing."*

If you take time to discuss the day with the class, the child will probably remember something to tell her parents.

Unfortunately, it won't always be something that reveals what a remarkable teacher you are. For example, one of my students proudly told her parents, "Today Mrs. Simmons taught me to walk on the right side of the hallway."

The Eighth Activity: Assigning Homework

Be sure that each child has a piece of work to take home to share with his parents. Perhaps this work can be expanded upon for a homework assignment. In grade 1, it might be an illustration and a one-line sentence that a child can read to a parent. For homework, the sentence might be copied. An older child might complete a set of math problems. For homework, he might write an original math story problem to share with the class the next day. Your explanation should include a review of homework guidelines.

Just Before Dismissal

Before dismissal, say a word or two to each child. It doesn't have to be profound, just personal, such as "I like the drawing you

made of your cat" or "Thank you for helping Sandy when she fell."
Then check to see that each child knows exactly how he's going
home and where he'll meet his parent or the bus. Accompany any
child who seems even remotely unsure or any child new to the
school.

As You Walk Home

As you walk home from school, you'll find yourself reflecting
on the day. You may ask yourself:

Were there alternating quiet and active times?

Was there a balance between formal and informal instruction?

Did the children have time to work together in a group?

Did the children have time to work independently?

Overall, were the children relaxed and involved?

Allow yourself to kick up your heels and say "Wow! I made it
through the first day!"

SOCIALIZING THE CHILD

As a teacher of young children, it is your responsibility to have
good manners yourself and to make the children aware of good
manners. If parents do their part of the job, you'll reinforce what's
being taught at home. If parents are neglectful, you'll have to
shoulder this job alone, and it's doubly important that you do
it well.

Courtesy

Do rules of courtesy inhibit the expression of natural feeling?
Yes.

Do they emphasize values that are conventional and behavior that's artificial? Yes.

Are they absolutely necessary for civilized living? Yes!

Rules of courtesy are like traffic signs; they remind us when to stop and when to go. They also prevent accidents. In another sense, rules of courtesy are like well-placed lamps: they help us see others in a better light.

Three basic rules for school are:

1. Say "please" and "thank you." These words are ways of acknowledging that others don't have an obligation to serve us. If we want their attention, we should ask for it politely. If we get their help, we should thank them.

2. Be considerate. If Gloria is standing alone in the playground, go over and ask her if she wants to join you on the monkey bars. If Tim is out of the room during snack time, save a cookie for him. If Eddie's bookbag is missing, offer to help him find it.

3. Don't interrupt. When *you* talk, you expect others to listen; when *they* talk, they expect you to listen. If you interrupt them, they feel rejected and insulted. Furthermore, if you don't listen to others, you can't learn from them!

But don't go to extremes. Being considerate doesn't mean sacrificing yourself for someone else; it means being helpful, within reason.

Conversation

Conversation is talk, not in public with the entire class, but in private with a few friends or just one. The purpose of conversation is sharing. Thus the key questions are, "What do *you* think?" and "How do *you* feel about that?" If one child does all the talking and another all the listening, that's not conversation—it's domination.

The content of conversation varies. You want to encourage the exchange of information, ideas, and feelings. You want to discourage chatter. (Chatter is silly talk such as "Milk tastes yucky. Lettuce tastes yucky. Furniture tastes yucky!" These memorable words are usually followed by giggling, which is then followed by rolling on the floor. The point of all this? To avoid working, of course.)

Personal Appearance

You don't want children to "dress up" for school as if they're going to a party. But you *do* want them to be clean, neat, and comfortably dressed in clothes that are appropriate for the classroom and for that day's weather. You want this, not only because it's esthetically pleasing to you and to others, but because experience has shown that a child who's properly groomed will feel better about himself and behave better in class than a child who looks dirty and sloppy.

Proper grooming means that children arrive with their hands and faces washed, their nails cleaned, their hair combed, and their teeth brushed. (If a child has braces, it means that he'll have to brush his teeth after snacks and lunch. You should see to it, of course, that he can do this in privacy, without calling undue attention to himself.)

Naturally, as the day wears on, children will probably get dirt on their pants, tomato juice on their shirts, and paint in their hair. That's normal. (Incidentally, to get paint out of hair, use mayonnaise. It works like magic!)

Appropriate dress means that shoelaces will be tied and that light clothing will be worn in hot weather and warm clothing in cold weather.

Personal Hygiene

When a nose is dripping, you have to insist
That it doesn't get wiped on a cuff or a wrist!

THE END OF THE FIRST WEEK

You'll probably feel overwhelmed and exhausted at the end of the first week. But we hope you'll also feel pleased about your first official week in the classroom as a "real" teacher. You should— you've just passed a milestone in your life! As a first-year teacher once put it, "The difference between taking education courses and teaching is the difference between packing a parachute and jumping."

The weekend will give you a chance to replenish your energy and plan for the coming week. It's time to put some distance between yourself and the intense experiences you've had in school. Treat yourself by doing something that's relaxing and lighthearted.

Before planning for the second week, reflect on what was comfortable for you in your classroom and on what wasn't. Expect that there'll be need for improvement and that it's natural and inevitable that you'll be continually reworking and refining your program.

As you observed the children during the first week, you became aware of their different styles of learning. You noticed that some children remembered best what they *read*, others what they *wrote down*, and still others what they *heard or repeated aloud*. Now is a good time to make notes about the visual, kinesthetic, and auditory strengths and weaknesses of each child. This information, in conjunction with their previous learning profiles, will guide you in your approach to teaching each child.

Finally, as you look ahead to the second week, you'll want to choose a theme that can be the basis for the first unit of the year. The best theme is one that the children have discovered themselves; it insures their interest and helps to bond the class ("We're doing *our* theme!"). There's plenty of time later to follow a prescribed curriculum.

3
Planning for the
Second Week of School

Photograph by Jack Kausch/Courtesy of Cranbrook Educational Community

REACHING OUT TO EACH CHILD

Individualized Activities

Identify the children at each end of the range of achievement so that you can motivate and challenge the high achiever as well as give extra support and help to the child who doesn't learn as quickly or has a special need.

Early in the year you might want to start a "Student of the Week" program. In this program, each child is assigned a week to share his life and interests with his teacher and classmates. In Mrs. Golden's first-grade classroom, for example, the "Student of the Week" was selected by drawing a name out of a hat. The child and the class were then involved all week in many activities chosen by the "Student of the Week." The spotlight was on that child for the entire week. During this time, the student might

make a poster of photographs featuring her family and family occasions.

O nce, a classmate looked intently at such a poster and asked Julie, the Student of the Week, "How old is your mother?"
Julie thought and thought and finally said, "She's either 37 or 73!"

plan a bulletin board with a "This-Is-My-Life" theme.

paint a life-size portrait of herself with the help of her classmates.

invite Mom and Dad to school to talk about their occupations.

take the class on a field trip to the parents' place of work.

invite grandparents to share slides and memories.

*O*nce, *a grandmother came to school wearing an unusual fur coat. Six-year-old Robin just loved it. She took every opportunity to rub up against it and stroke it.*
Finally, she asked, "What kind of fur is your coat?"
When the grandmother said the fur was rabbit, Robin's eyes opened wide. "How big was that rabbit?"

For the higher grades, you might want to have a "Student of the Day," following a similar format. In this instance, the student might

bring a pet to school.

display a collection.

make a slide show of a trip.

perform a musical piece on an instrument.

write and illustrate his own book.

Small-Group Activities

Informally chart the range of ability of the group. Use pre-tests to help in placement (published pre-tests or informal teacher-written surveys may be used). If further evaluation seems necessary, call upon resource teachers.

Plan when you'll be working with different groups and what productive activity the rest of the children will be doing during this time. Check to see that you have materials to cover all ranges. Match special activities and services to specific children.

This is a tall order. The familiar cry of new teachers is, "How can I be everywhere at once?" The answer is, you don't have to be if you prepare thoroughly and recognize that each small-group instruction period has seven parts:

Part 1: Divide the class into several groups—four seems to be a workable number—assigning each child to Group A,

B, C, or D, according to his ability, which you've gauged from reading and skill tests.

Part 2: Assign each group a project appropriate to its abilities. For example:

Group A: The children will read the story "The Popcorn Dragon," under your guidance.

Group B: The children will go to the Listening Post, where they'll listen and read along with the story "Ping." Then they'll write a new ending to the story (using a minimum of four sentences) and illustrate the ending.

Group C: The children will work on suffixes in their phonics books, filling in the blanks on pages 29–31. Then they'll put their books in the box labeled "Completed Work" so that you can mark it.

Group D: The children will write ten funny sentences using the words in the weekly spelling list.

Of course, there will always be some children who have difficulty working alone or following an assignment. They may need more specific directions or definite assurance that they're doing what's expected of them. Because you don't want to be interrupted, pair these children with "helping buddies" or seat them at a table with a child who has a teaching instinct. If all else fails, let them know they can come to you during switching of groups.

Part 3: List on the chalkboard the follow-up activity for each group. For example:

When Group A finishes reading "The Popcorn Dragon" under your guidance, they'll go to a far corner of the room, where they'll dramatize the story. (Appoint one child to be "Director." Also, if you feel that a certain child in this group is likely to be disruptive, give him a quiet assignment at his desk or at the Listening Post.)

When Group B finishes at the Listening Post, they'll have free time to work on their book reports.

When Group C finishes their work in the phonics book, they'll come to your table for vocabulary drill with flash cards.

When Group D finishes writing their funny sentences, they'll go to the computers (which have signs that say "No more than two children at each computer").

Incidentally, to keep the room from getting noisy or chaotic, be sure that you never have more than *two* groups functioning as *groups* at any given time.

And to keep yourself from becoming frustrated, accept the fact that you aren't Super Teacher. Ideally, you should be able to give your personal attention to all four groups during this period, but realistically, you'll be doing well if you personally supervise *two* groups.

Part 4: List on the chalkboard the free-choice alternatives for anyone who completes *all* assigned activities. For example:

Paint a picture.
Read a new magazine.
Use an available computer or Listening Post.

Inevitably, some children won't be finished when the period ends.

Part 5: Remind them that there'll be "special time" during the week to complete unfinished work, and that some work can be done at home. (But be sure that no child is overloaded with home assignments.)

Part 6: Now gather the class together and let the children in Group A present their dramatization, the children in

Group B read their new endings and show their illustrations, and the children in Group D share their funny sentences.

If there isn't time for all this—and there usually isn't—then these activities can begin the next day's small-group period.

Part 7: Plan to correct and return independent work as soon as possible. If you delay more than three days, the children won't take future assignments seriously because they'll conclude that you don't really consider such assignments important.

Although marking papers is tedious, it will give you valuable information. You'll know which child needs to be challenged, which one needs to repeat an assignment, and which one needs to work with you. It may even indicate that a certain child needs to be moved from one group to another.

Obviously, maneuvering among four small groups requires artful navigation. Don't expect to master this skill overnight. If you see that you're heading for the rocks, come about and take a new tack.

You'll always find clear sailing if you bring the children together and introduce a new activity that involves the entire class. And remember this: Usually everything jells by March (sometimes even sooner)!

Homework

Think of homework as a review and another way to help build study skills and habits. It also has a third purpose: to let parents know what's being studied in the classroom and to invite them to participate in their child's learning.

When you're planning homework, establish the purpose of the assignment and spell out your expectations. Be sure to make this clear to the students.

Homework assignments are most effective when they grow out of classroom lessons and units of study. These assignments may vary from the ordinary, such as studying spelling words, to the more creative, such as making a sun dial.

For older children, a monthly calendar of due dates is helpful. (An individual assignment book helps children to be better organized.)

Be aware of the appropriate length of time for an age group or individual child to complete a homework assignment. For example, if the assignment should take 20 minutes, some children will complete it in 10 minutes and others in 30 minutes. If a child is taking two hours, that's not productive! The parents should be instructed to set time limits for their children, even if the assignment is not completed.

The entire subject of homework was treated very shrewdly by our colleague, Andrew Mulligan:

A good way to judge if a boy is learning or not is by his daily homework. You'll be surprised how much it can tell. If he doesn't understand the material covered in class or the assignment, his homework will reflect that. It'll be messy, poorly written, full of mistakes, have lots of unfinished problems, or worse, it will not have been done at all.

I used to think there was no excuse for missed homework. I was wrong. There are lots of excuses.

Just last week a boy told me the reason he didn't have his homework was because his father had it.

"Really?"

"Yeah. My dad liked it so much he took it to work to show his boss."

"And his boss found it interesting?"

"Oh, yeah."

I closed my eyes to indicate my disbelief.

"Henry, do you remember the subject of that assignment?"
"Sure. Describe the smell of a locker room."

A LETTER TO PARENTS

During the first week of school, the administration irons out the kinks in overall scheduling. Once this has been done, you can send a letter to parents welcoming them to your grade, describing your program, and letting them in on some of the plans that are in store for them and their children.

In this letter you also can answer questions that you know parents have been dying to ask you, such as those relating to homework procedures or needed equipment. (You may say, "But I already told the children to tell their parents, and I already sent a notice home with each child." But what if the child forgot to tell them—and she will! And what if the notice never got home—and it won't!) To be safe, *mail the letter.*

There is, of course, no standard format to follow. Here, for your guidance, is a sample letter that we used one year in second grade.

Dear Parents,

Welcome to Second Grade! We are looking forward to an enjoyable year, and have many programs and special activities planned for your child.

Homeroom Program: *Reading, writing, and mathematics will be covered every day in the homeroom; art, creative writing, literature, and social science will be an integral part of the daily homeroom program.*

Enrichment Program:

Physical		
Education	*Mrs. Lusk/Mr. Brown*	*5 times per week*
Music	*Mrs. Tower*	*4 times per week*

Science	Mr. Schultz	3 times per week
Reading		
Enrichment	Mrs. McClear/Mr. Jenkins	As necessary
Library	Mrs. Stone	Once a week
Drama	Mrs. Roberts	Once a week
Health Care	Mrs. Smart	Once a week

Homework: *To encourage the growth of positive study habits, we feel the children should be responsible for some homework each school night. To help the children develop a routine, it is advisable to establish a specific place and time for work. There will be three homework assignments daily.*

1. *A written task in one of the academic subjects. This should take 10–15 minutes to complete.*

2. *Every Monday your child will bring home spelling sentences and spelling words for nightly study. This study period should take 10–15 minutes. At the beginning of the year it's a good idea to help your child—especially on Wednesday, since every Thursday there will be a spelling test in class.*

3. *To stimulate reading for pleasure on a regular basis, we encourage a 15-minute reading period nightly. Your child may choose to read independently or may read aloud to a member of the family.*

Personal Equipment: *Your child will need a smock for art activities, a pair of tennis shoes to be used during physical education, and an extra sweater (to be left at school) for the soon-to-be-cold weather. Please make sure all items are clearly marked with your child's name. Starting in December the Second Grade will go ice skating one morning a week at the Cranbrook Skating Rink. One of our staff members, Mrs. Geoghegan (who is a professional skating instructor), will give group instruction. You may want to think ahead about getting skates for your child.*

Trips: This year we are planning several trips to the nature center at the Cranbrook Institute of Science. We have many exciting ideas for other field trips and will announce them as soon as arrangements are completed.

Ice Skating

I remember when we went skating the first time. We went to the ice rink by bus. The bus drive was short, only about three minutes. At first I fell a lot but later I could skate better and I didn't fall as much. We sometimes played tag and had races. After skating we had snack. Then we got on the bus and went back to school.

By Carlo

Open House: *We will talk about our program in greater depth at the Open House on September 27th. At that time we will be happy to answer any further questions you may have.*

Sincerely,

Dee Appleman
Sharon Cooper

LEARNING CENTERS

The Philosophy of Learning Centers

Learning centers are areas in the classroom designated for the study of specific subjects—for example, a quiet, private area for a Reading Center, and a spacious area for math, to allow for free use of building and measuring materials. Another corner of the room is set aside for displaying projects, which may stay up for a week, or, depending on student interest, for as long as a month.

T   *he children were assigned to read a biography. Several of them, who read about Thomas Edison, became so excited that they decided to put up a display of Edison's life, including photographs of him, his workshop, and his many inventions, such as the electric light bulb, the phonograph, and the motion picture projector. Randolph even displayed an invention of his own—Randolph's Special Spaghetti Fork!*

And that, really, is the reason for a learning center: to stimulate children to work creatively. (A secondary benefit is that, when a child is working on his own, it teaches him to concentrate on the book or project in front of him while the rest of the class is busy doing other things. This is a valuable skill, since a student rarely has ideal study conditions at home, in school, or later in college.)

For a detailed discussion of the eight learning centers in our classroom—Reading, Audio-Visual, Writing, Math, Computer, Art, Pet, Science—see Appendix A. We advise you to read this appendix after you've finished the entire book and when you have time to devote exclusively to this large subject.

Chapter

4
Planning Enrichment Projects

Photograph by Richard Hirneisen/Courtesy of Cranbrook Educational Community

ONGOING UNITS

You've launched the school year. You're acquainted with your children and are beginning to know their levels and interests. They can't wait for the real exciting "work" to begin, so choose a theme—one that can be expanded to last two or three weeks.

Perhaps you'll have the class observe the seasonal changes from summer to autumn: the ripening of fruits, the sluggishness of insects, the changing colors of the landscape.

I used to begin the year in second grade with a unit on the behavior of bees. Our school is in the suburbs, but it feels as if we're nestled in the country. Just when we begin school, we see bees throughout the grounds.

Some children are afraid, others are curious—but all are very much aware of the bees' presence. Therefore, it's a perfect subject for the first unit. And it offers children an opportunity to explore, question and confront a genuine concern.

Sometimes we begin by reading an excerpt from Winnie-the-Pooh, *because, as we all know, Pooh is a great lover of honey. ("And the only reason for making honey is so I can eat it.")*

Once we're thinking and talking about bees, I ask the children what they know about these insects. It turns out they know a lot, and the more they know, the more questions they have.

You can begin the unit by listing their questions:

How do bees know how to build honeycombs?

What does their dance mean?

Are there different dances?

What's a beeline?

How many queen bees are in a hive?

You have the beginning of a unit, chosen to fit the interests of your children. Now plan something to study or do in all areas of the curriculum for the next few weeks.

Science: Our school is located near a science institute that features a honey harvest in September. We walk there, and the children can actually observe bees on the path from the flower to the hive. They watch the bees through a glass hive, looking for the queen bee, the worker bees, and the drones. With the help of a naturalist, they extract the honey from the honeycomb and taste it! When we return to school, each child draws a diagram of the hive and lists the various jobs of the different bees.

Language arts: In addition to reading books and magazines and writing logs of their experience at the institute, the children work on crossword puzzles, using vocabulary from the unit. They use words they've collected such as *workers, nectar, drone, hive, soldier, dance,* and *bodies.* These words can also be used as the spelling words of the week; the children will need to know them for various writing projects.

Math: The children learn to construct 120-degree angles, such as the ones they examined in the cells of the hive. They look for this shape in nature, in their homes, and in pictures. This is exciting and shows that math is more than just computation.

The children also measure ingredients for recipes, making a snack of honey mousse, honey cake, honey jam, or honey nut balls. Mothers can help with these projects and they love to!

The most important long-range goal to set early in the year is the creation of an atmosphere in which children are excited about learning and can grow to feel a mastery over a subject. The greater the involvement, the more lasting the learning will be.

There are many tools you can use to achieve this goal, such as carefully selected books, interesting bulletin board displays, visual and auditory aids, and of course, best of all, first-hand experience!

Short Trips (No Travel Preparations)

Spontaneous short trips are best because they grow out of the need of the moment. You don't have to make elaborate plans and you don't have to prepare the class—you just go! It's interesting and adds spice to the day!

A wonderful book that suggests such trips and how they happen is *A Teacher's Guide, Ten-Minute Field Trips (Using the School Grounds for Environmental Studies)* by Helen Ross Russell. This book offers fascinating information about the outdoor world in city and country, and excellent techniques to keep children's attention and interest.

*M*any studies require ongoing observation and record-keeping such as temperature comparisons. Keep a thermometer outside the classroom door or window and the students will be able to gather information under different weather conditions.

Have the children circle a tree so they can make observations from all vantage points. Have them take a census of the animals that are using the tree for food or shelter.

Later they may sit in a circle on the lawn where each child can see and hear the others as they discuss their discoveries.

Some other trip books by Helen Ross Russell are

Soil: A Field Trip Guide

Winter: A Field Trip Guide

Small Worlds: A Field Trip Guide

Most of these trips are related to scientific investigation, but with a little ingenuity you can do the same sort of thing in history or writing.

All-Day Trips (Away from School Grounds)

Longer trips will require pre-planning:

Do you have a blanket permission form, signed by the parents, to take their child on *all* trips? Or do you need a separate permission slip for *each* trip?

Will the children need money or a bag lunch? (If they need a bag lunch, take trash bags along. If they need money, how much is needed and who will handle it?)

What's appropriate dress for that day? (For example, if children are going to a sheep farm, they'll need boots.)

How will you get to where you're going? (Plan for bus or car transportation, and make sure that the vehicle has seat belts. This will determine the number of children riding in that vehicle.)

How many adults do you need to accompany you? (Remember that parents often feel nervous when they're responsible for other people's children. It helps to provide each parent with a packet containing a map and the names of the children in his or her group.)

What services are available for children at this place? Where will coats be hung? Can the children eat lunch there? Where are the bathrooms located?

What are the requirements of the place you're visiting? Can the children touch any of the objects on display? Will there be someone around to explain the exhibit? What would be an appropriate noise level?

How will you work out a buddy system? Will you honor
children's requests for partners? What about the child who is
left over if there's an uneven number? Will you pair the more
active children with the quieter ones? Will you keep the less
mature children near you or will you assign them to a parent?

Preparing the Children

Make the purpose of the trip clear to the class.
Children must be well prepared for a trip if it's going to be a
really valuable learning experience.

Students must be told to look for specific things.
(For example, at the planetarium they can look for a display that
highlights the red spot of Jupiter.) But children need to do something besides look, because some won't retain what they see and
others will get into trouble when they're just looking.

Older children may be given pencil-and-paper assignments. For
example, they might

fill out answers on a prepared fill-in sheet.

record observations about x.

compare x and y.

follow a map and check off what they've seen.

Review Rules of Behavior
On the day before the trip, sit down with the class and go over
the rules of behavior. You might, for example, want to remind
them that

you should be able to see them at all times.

they must *always* let you know if they're going to leave your
sight to get a drink.

you'll use a silent signal—raising your right hand high—to get
their attention.

they must stay with their assigned buddy and adult supervisor.

you expect them to be courteous to their classmates and to everyone else.

Dress
Unless it's an outdoor trip, encourage the children to dress up. Somehow, when they're dressed up, they feel better and act better.

The Day of the Trip

Be at school early in case you have to prepare last-minute materials or a child needs special attention for some reason. (Maybe there's a child who hasn't returned a permission note and you'll

a Sheep Farm

We went to a sheep farm in February. We all went in four big white vans. We didn't see any having babies. It was a long drive, but we got there. We jumped on haystacks. They told us they had 500 sheep. We went on a hay ride that was fun!

by Tony

have to arrange for someone to phone the parent for permission. If you can't reach the parent, you'll have to arrange for a place for the child to spend the day. In addition, you'll have to soothe his disappointed feelings.)

Wear comfortable, cheerful clothing. Review plans and expectations with the children (without the parents around to distract them). Review the purpose of the trip. Be sure that each child has used the bathroom before you leave. Answer last-minute questions. Take a head count. And finally, *leave on a note of enthusiasm.*

<u>Earth Men Fly to the Moon</u>

Our class did a unit on space. We wrote reports on the subject. We went to the Planetarium. Boy was that fun!!! You can see stars and planets and constellations. Why, we even made a space ship!!! Mine had an engine. (A missile too!!!) I learned that Jupiter's red spot is as big as two earths and if Jupiter was just a little bigger it would be a Star.

by Will

If You Run into Trouble

A trip can be a horrible experience or a treasured one, depending on how the children behave on the day of the trip. Children rarely are discipline problems when they're interested in what they're doing, but sometimes in a new situation an immature child can be very naughty, enticing others to join him.

If this happens and you find yourself beginning to feel uncomfortable, don't be afraid to stop everything. Call the class together and wait for everyone's undivided attention (no matter how long it takes and no matter how many parents or strangers are looking on). Then make it very clear, in a quiet but firm voice, that the class's behavior is unacceptable and that there will be consequences. It isn't a good idea to threaten children, but on occasion it's necessary and effective.

If you misjudge a situation and it's not the children's fault that things are going wrong, then think quickly, be creative, take control, and reverse your plans.

We took a group of fifth-graders to the Detroit Institute of Art.

The children had been well prepared. In addition to discussions about the history and art on display, the Social Studies teacher had gone to great pains to compose two sheets of fill-ins for the children to use as they walked through the exhibit.

When we got to the museum, we discovered that the show was in several small rooms. This meant that all fifty fifth-graders couldn't possibly fit in the space surrounding the first object listed on the fill-in. As they crowded together, mass confusion resulted.

We knew we had to change our plans on the spot or else the experience would be a fiasco.

Then and there, right in the middle of the exhibit, we got the children to sit down on the floor. The teachers had a quick meeting. We decided to collect all papers and pencils (alas, so much work down the drain), divide the children into small groups assigned to an adult, and stagger the groups throughout the rooms.

By having the courage to admit we had made a mistake, we were able to salvage the day, and provide an extraordinary experience for both adults and children.

HOLIDAYS

When we were children in the elementary grades, Thanksgiving meant paper turkeys and Christmas meant a three-dimensional Christmas tree. This was fun for us because we didn't get to do art projects very often, but it didn't address the meaning of the holiday.

Holidays are more than days off from school and the study of dates, facts, and symbols. They are celebrations that occur over and over throughout a lifetime. From an early age children learn what's coming next and begin to look forward to these special occasions. In addition, children tend to feel safe and happy in a school environment where ceremonies are respected and traditions are repeated.

Halloween

Halloween is usually the first holiday in our school when all the children come together. It's the least serious but the most colorful and exciting holiday of the year (especially for the younger children who aren't really sure that goblins, ghosts, and witches aren't real). Children, teachers, and parents all take part in the festivities. As you can imagine, parents are the most appreciative audiences in the world.

The younger children can't wait to put on their costumes. They dress first thing in the morning, then they parade in the gymnasium for the older children and their own parents. The little ones in their bunny, Superman, and ballerina costumes are so adorable that even the blasé fifth-graders melt when they walk by.

In the afternoon, the older children parade for the younger ones. The little ones sit open-mouthed and gaze with admiration at the parade of TV personalities, monsters, and sexy teenagers.

Teachers are part of the scene, too! (One of the most worrisome problems of the year for a teacher is "What will I be for Halloween?" Teachers have solved this problem in a variety of creative ways. We've had Cookie Monsters, walking Christmas trees with flashing Christmas lights, and last year, the art teacher was a most convincing gnome!)

It's a time of good sportsmanship, creativity, and camaraderie.

The Halloween Parade

One day on October 29th the Brookside School had a Halloween Parade. There were E.T.'s and witches all over the place. We had a lot of fun. Sean was Dracula. Riley was a flower in a basket. Kristen L. was an angel, and I was a witch.

Tanya

Thanksgiving

At the beginning of the year, each class adopts a "grandparent," with the help of a local agency that provides meals and books to older people who live alone. From early September through mid-November, the children write letters and send drawings and photographs to this person. When Thanksgiving arrives, we invite the "grandparent" to come to school for morning tea and a Thanksgiving program. (Of course we also include the children's own grandparents.)

Several teachers volunteer to pick up the guests. This can be complicated, because many of these older people are confined to wheelchairs. But their smiles and obvious pleasure make it all worthwhile.

The Piano Lady

Mrs. Joslyn is a lady who came to our school for Thanksgiving. She played the piano for us and we all sang songs. And I will tell you a secret that you would never guess, Mrs. Joslyn is blind.

by Don

*M*rs. Joslyn, one of our "adopted grandparents," lost her sight gradually as she aged. Before this happened, she was a piano teacher. But, as if by magic, she still plays beautifully.

When she comes to school, we make sure there's a piano available so that the children can gather around her to sing holiday songs. When she leaves, the children can't stop talking about the fact that, even though she's blind, she never misses a note!

Christmas

On December 1st, I go to my storage room to get the plywood dollhouse that I put away so carefully after Christmas last year. Then I tiptoe into my classroom and display it in the center of the room. Of course the children are curious, so I tell them that in a few days we're going to make a candy house.

They immediately begin to chatter about the best way to decorate it and, as the days pass, the excitement mounts! Finally D-Day (Decorating Day) comes. I gather all the ingredients and we begin to make the mortar (frosting) to cover the house. The children beat the eggs, add some cream of tartar, sprinkle in confectioner's sugar, mix everything, and paint the house with the frosting.

Then out come the trays of hard candies, chocolate bars, candy canes, string licorice—all the ingredients for a holiday masterpiece! In a matter of seconds, the plain wooden structure is transformed into a fantasy house. You can hear "oohs" and "aahs" from all around the room. Soon the word gets around school and children of all ages are peeping through the door to see the "wonder."

Now comes the long-awaited moment. The class takes the prized possession to a nearby nursing home and the children proudly wheel the brightly colored house on a cart through the rooms, picking choice treats from the house to give to all the residents. Some children are talkative and affectionate, others are a little shy and mostly watch. Feelings can't be measured, but for all of us it's a day we'll remember.

Valentine's Day

Each child has his very own homemade mailbox, usually decorated with hearts and flowers. The box is placed in a prominent place. Children make or buy valentines for everyone in their class and drop them in the mailboxes sometime before February 14th. This means that everyone is guaranteed at least twenty valentines, plus any others he might receive from children in other classes or from teachers (most get at least thirty-five).

The instructions are to open each card slowly, think about the person who gave it to you, and savor the pleasure of having been remembered with so much affection. No one ever seems to realize that *everyone* gets a lot of cards. All a child knows is that he does, and he feels *very, very* popular.

This is the sweetest, most intimate holiday of all—truly a children's holiday!

Ethnic Holidays

Although many holidays have religious roots, they can still be celebrated in school as historical and ethnic holidays. A child feels

Matzo and Butter

On Passover, they served matzo and butter for lunch. I didn't think I would like it. But it was so delicious, I had seconds!

by Jody

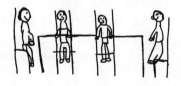

so proud when her holiday (which in her mind stands for *her*) is recognized and respected.

Naturally you can't spend time on every single ethnic holiday, but it *is* appropriate to learn about those that are relevant to your school population. If you have Oriental children, you'll want to include the Chinese New Year, and if you have Jewish children, plan for Chanukah and Passover. Parents can be really helpful, and they are usually thorough in their preparation.

*D*uring the week of Passover, we change the lunch menu, leave out foods that Jewish children aren't allowed to eat, and introduce some of the traditional Passover foods.
It's always amazing that the non-Jewish children can't seem to get enough matzo and butter!

Chapter

5
Goals for the
First Three Months

Photograph by Taro Yamasaki/Courtesy of Cranbrook Educational Community

SETTING A TONE FOR YOUR CLASSROOM

Turning Fog into Fairyland

Inevitably, there'll be days of rain, fog, sleet, snow, or bitter cold. Just as inevitably, some children will reflect the blue mood of the weather by complaining, whining, and being out of sorts.

R*uth was moping because it was very foggy and she was sure recess would have to be cancelled. Soon, other children were making a fuss, and I had to respond.*

It was obvious that I couldn't do anything about the fog, but I could do something about their attitude. I could try to make the fog interesting, to turn their annoyance into fascination.

I gathered everyone in the story corner and read them Carl Sandburg's poem "Fog."

*The fog comes
on little cat feet.*

*It sits looking
over harbor and city
on silent haunches
and then moves on.*

The children looked out the window as they listened to the poem. Then they read the poem to themselves. Then we chanted it together, softly.

Moments later, we tiptoed out into the fog to experience the beauty of the soft and silent morning.

When we returned to the room, we were all excited. The children began to write down their thoughts about the fog. Some wrote poems, others stories, others told me what they were thinking and I wrote it down. Some drew misty pictures.

*Everyone hoped for another foggy morning soon . . .
but before that happened, there was the magic of the first
snowflake!*

The climate outside is Nature's responsibility; the climate in the
classroom is yours.

Your Manner

The children will mirror a pleasant personality, so try to

smile often and genuinely.

place a gentle hand on a child to re-establish attention.

give support with physical contact. If a child is receptive,
give hugs.

make yourself accessible. Move about the room, giving the
children individual help and encouragement.

be enthusiastic, especially when introducing a new subject or
activity, or when a child achieves a goal.

handle awkward or stressful situations with humor. (When a
softball takes a bad bounce and hits a little boy in the chest
and he begins to cry, you'll be tempted to say, "Oh, that must
hurt something awful." But such consolation will probably
make him cry harder. The response that ends the tears and
brings a smile is, "That happens to the best of shortstops. Last
week I saw it happen to Alan Trammell!")

Your Voice

Your voice is the connecting link between you and the class.
Some children complain that their teacher has a **HARSH** voice
that sounds unfriendly or a *borrring* voice that puts them to sleep.
Here are some ways to make your voice more pleasant and
effective.

Speak clearly enough to be heard in all corners of the room. But don't shout. When your voice gets loud, the children's voices get louder.

Avoid an angry tone; if necessary, speak sternly in a low voice.

Look directly at the child you're talking to. Don't talk too much.

Your Tolerance for Noise

Teachers vary in their tolerance for noise. You must find a level that's both comfortable for you and normal for healthy, active children! You can expect a hum in the room when the children are engaged in art projects, cooking projects, block building, and small-group planning sessions.

If the noise rises to an inappropriate level, stop the activity until the room becomes quiet. If the noise rises again, it may indicate the need for a change of activity.

Rewards versus Bribes

A reward is a prize given for exceptional effort. A bribe is an inducement to get a child to do what he *should* do.

A reward is educationally sound. On the other hand, a bribe teaches a child two terrible lessons: (1) that nothing is expected of him and (2) that adults are willing to pay a ransom for almost anything.

Being Fair

The do's

The tone of civility in a classroom depends, above all, on the children's feeling that you're a fair person. Let them know that you may not be able to act with perfect fairness every moment of every day, but assure them that over the course of the year you'll try to give fair attention, affection, and recognition to everyone.

Also assure them that, if you have to arbitrate a dispute, you'll do so fairly and will expect them to accept your decision with good grace and without lingering resentment.

The don'ts

Don't play favorites.

Don't establish out-of-school relationships with children in your class. It tends to cause jealousy. ("Mrs. A. went to Sheila's house. Why didn't she come to mine? She likes Sheila better. I hate Sheila.")

Don't patronize a child from a disadvantaged background or criticize the values of a child from an affluent background. Instead, help each child to appreciate the positive aspects of his own life and at the same time open windows that look out on other values and other achievements.

Don't forget that your perception of fairness may sometimes be quite different from a student's.

*L*aurent's teacher didn't pronounce Laurent's name exactly as Laurent preferred. Laurent thought about this a lot, but his teacher didn't. Instead, his teacher thought about how to get Laurent to do the "right" thing at the "right" time, for Laurent could never bear to leave a game or project that he was involved in. Consequently, he was never there when the other children were ready for lunch or a story or recess.

Finally, his teacher decided that the situation had to be handled in a way that would appeal to Laurent's imagination. He gave Laurent a string to carry in his pocket, saying, "I want you to put a knot in this string every time you aren't ready for a class activity. Then, at the end of the week, we'll examine the string to see how many knots are in it." Laurent liked the idea of the game and was a willing participant.

At the end of the week, his teacher said, "Laurent, let's see how that string is doing." Laurent nodded, and took the string out of his pocket. There were many knots in it. Before his teacher could make any comment, Laurent took a second string from his pocket with just as many knots in it. "What's that?" his teacher asked. Laurent replied, "That's how many times this week you didn't remember to say my name right."

EFFECTIVE COMMUNICATION

Getting the Children's Attention

Be sure you have everyone's attention before you begin a lesson. Even if it takes a little while, wait for the student who isn't ready.

Use signals, such as dimming the lights, holding up one arm in Scout style, or standing still in a part of the room where most of the children will notice you. The group will pass the word along that you have something to say.

When you speak, use a statement rather than a question. If you say "May I have your attention?" the group will probably shout back "No!" It's better to say, "Please pay attention."

Giving Instructions

At the beginning of the year, give only one instruction at a time. In September, you might say "Please come to the Writing Center. All the materials you need are already there." Later in the year, as the children mature and become more careful listeners, you can say "Please come to the Writing Center, and bring your pencil, your journal, your personal dictionary, and your crayons."

Use silent signals to avoid interruptions. For example, a child can be taught to hold up his "pointer" finger if he wants to leave the room to go to the bathroom. You can acknowledge this signal with a simple nod of the head.

Avoid questions that encourage a group response, such as "Who wants to go to recess?" Instead, say "As soon as your desks are cleared, we'll go to recess."

Giving Criticism

Try to avoid singling anyone out for criticism. Instead, make a general positive statement to the group, such as "I like the way Billy is quietly reading his story." With luck, the child who isn't reading will settle down to work. If this doesn't happen, take him aside and have a private talk.

Don't get into an argument with a child.

Recognize when a child is testing you or when he's such an individualist that he finds it hard to accept orders meant for a group.

*S*teven was a charming seven-year-old. He was *strong-willed, determined, and an independent thinker.*

Quite often, when an instruction was given to the class, such as "Find six items in the room to measure," Steven would say, "But . . ." Then he'd try to revise the instructions. "Can't we measure things outside the room, too? Why don't we measure just five items?"

Or if Steven was asked to join a group, he'd say "But . . . but I have to finish writing my story. I'll be there in a few minutes."

One day I thought of a ploy that might make Steven see that his buts weren't appropriate. When he raised his hand to ask if he could leave the room, I said, "I'd certainly like to let you go, but I have to finish marking these papers first."

A child like Steven usually perseveres in the hope that you'll give in from exhaustion. Say "no," be firm, but also be sensitive if you're working with someone who occasionally needs the option of an alternative.

Try not to get into a power struggle where there'll be a winner and loser. And try to avoid being drawn into an argument in front of the group. Postpone confronting the issue for a time when you can sit down alone with the student and talk.

Of course, when all is said and done, a teacher is only human, as, on occasion, even a student will realize.

One afternoon, Kate's teacher had had it. The day had been a series of disasters: spilled paint, broken toys, unsettled arguments, and ignored directions. Suddenly the teacher exploded with loud orders for a prompt, organized, thorough clean-up!

Kate looked up in surprise. "Well, I'll be. I never knew Teacher could get mad as hell!"

Dealing with Problems at Recess

Be supportive of children who can't find a friend or a group at recess. They'll probably come over to talk to you. Chat with them a bit, then ease them away from your side and get them involved with another child or group.

Children sometimes get into arguments during recess. Naturally, they come to the teacher to explain, often in tears. It's impossible to know who's right or wrong, so let both parties have turns voicing their complaints.

Talking gets the anger out. After awhile, step in and try to help the children find humor in the situation. Laughter and a handshake will usually follow as they skip off to play! Often the problem hasn't been resolved, but it doesn't seem to matter too much. While adults are left pondering these incidents, children quickly forget them.

Recess is usually a happy time and the majority of problems are resolved before you go back to the classroom. But if you notice a lingering effect later in the classroom, realize that more attention from you is necessary.

DEVELOPING A GROUP SPIRIT

A group spirit grows when each child feels good about identifying with the class, as a unit, in a positive way. Ideally, a person can remain an individual and yet function happily within the group.

Each group needs leaders and followers, and each individual needs the opportunity to play both roles. The goal is to encourage unique and creative thinking, and, at the same time, cooperation with the group.

To help students reach this goal,

encourage them to be tolerant of and interested in others—in their ideas, talents, and accomplishments. Guide children to appreciate and not minimize a fellow student's work.

help the class to develop positive ways of group expression and evaluation, such as complimenting and applauding, and to avoid negative verbal outbursts, such as booing.

plan group activities so that there's an opportunity for give and take. Sharing is one of the most important elements in setting classroom tone. Don't let a single, strong personality dominate the group.

make sure that bright children participate fully, to elevate the level of class discussion.

encourage children to feel pride in the accomplishments of the group: plays, fairs, exhibits, school teams. Discourage individual competitions such as racing through workbooks to be the first one finished.

The two group activities that most students experience with the greatest intensity are playing on a school athletic team and being in a theatrical production. These are one-for-all, all-for-one situations that develop exceptional camaraderie and loyalty. In addition, they focus on a single occasion when everything is at stake: winning or losing on the ballfield, success or failure on opening night. Such a challenge inspires a tremendous, unforgettable effort from all participants.

When people recall the big events of their early school years, they always wind up talking about their class plays.

*M*r. Blake's class was putting on a play, Ira Sleeps Over *(based on the book by Bernard Waber). The main character, Ira, is going to risk his first sleep-over date (with his friend, Reggie, who lives next door). Ira is excited, but he's also upset—because he's ashamed to take his teddy bear with him and he isn't sure he can fall asleep without it.*

He finally decides to be brave and try; but in the middle of the night, his bravery fails and he has to go across the lawn, back to his own house, to get his teddy bear. Fortunately, Reggie doesn't make fun of him because—guess what? Reggie sleeps with a teddy bear too!

Mr. Blake wanted all the children to feel involved in the play, so he decided to have a Teddy Bear Contest to choose Ira's teddy and Reggie's teddy. He asked each child to bring in his favorite bear.

The next morning 27 bears were lined up along the window ledge, where everyone could admire them. There were small ones, new ones, Smokeys from the forest, and Paddingtons from darkest Peru.

Naturally, everyone wanted his bear to win, but Mr. Blake asked the children to be fair and choose the ones that could be seen best from the audience. When it was time for the vote, Mr. Blake held them up one at a time, giving each one a special hug. After the two winners had been chosen, he congratulated the children on their good

Ira Sleeps Over

I remember when we did our play called "Ira Sleeps Over." I had two lines for Ira and one line for Reggie. For our scenery we had two houses, a gate, a chair, and two teddy bears. Our class painted Reggie's house and Mrs. Cooper's class painted Ira's. We also had a lot of instruments. I played the bass, mata-laphone. The play was about a boy named Ira who was afraid to take his teddy bear to sleep over. Our play was the best play. I loved it!

Reggy's teddy bear. Ira's teddy bear.

Reggie's house.

By Laura

taste and invited the other teddy bears to spend the rest of the week on the ledge in the dining room.

Some of these bears disappeared each afternoon and reappeared the next morning. Evidently, they couldn't sleep without their owners!

ESTABLISHING A RELATIONSHIP
WITH AN INDIVIDUAL CHILD

Recognize Each Child's Interests, Talents, and Needs

Because a child's day begins at home, he often arrives at school with feelings that need to be attended to before he's ready to begin work.

*J*on came to school teary-eyed some mornings. He had a baby sister at home, whom he missed terribly. He was also uncomfortable about the amount of attention she was getting from his mom when he was away.

To bridge the gap between home and school, and to help relieve Jon's anxious feelings, we decided that a visit from eight-month-old Jennifer would be a wonderful contribution to "Sharing Time." She was happy to come. She sat on the floor in the middle of a circle of children and cooed and giggled. We planned for her to visit once, but she was so popular she returned seven times, giving us a chance to watch her grow and change during the course of the year.

The class adopted her as the second-grade mascot, and Jon was the class hero!

As the year progresses, include moments with each student to review a homework assignment, to add a new word to a personal dictionary, to explore plans for a project, or to talk about a personal problem.

Be understanding of individual fears, such as the fear of insects, fire drills, doctors, or dentists.

Each child needs to feel your approval, so spread the favors around. You can do this by

Spoken words: suggestions, directions, expressions of interest or encouragement

Written words: positive comments on homework and class assignments, or a personal note left in a book or on a desk

Gestures: an OK sign, a wink of the eye, or a ready smile

Strokes: an affectionate pat on the head

Little gifts: a favorite sticker on a paper, a simple drawing, or a new pencil

Listening: take time to listen so that you can discover what's really bothering a child.

*I*t was a sad time for Naomi. Her mom and dad had decided to get a divorce. Naomi was to remain in Michigan with her father, while her mother and sister moved to Texas.

The move was scheduled to take place on the first of November. The day before, during the costume parade for the Halloween Party, Naomi was unusually quiet. Then suddenly she began to cry.

Between sobs, she stammered, "Who will help me make my costume next year? Mom is leaving, and dads can't do things like that!"

A Child Remembers

You can gauge how much you've helped a child learn by comparing his test scores and measuring his skills, but it's harder to measure the ways you've influenced his character and brought him joy. Yet as every teacher knows, the sweetest moments of your career are those when a student—months or even years later—reveals his affection and gratitude for some action that you barely remember but that he's never forgotten.

I was reminded of this when I read Paul's story, in his Memory Book, about his visit to Mr. Jenkins' apple orchard.

The Apple Orchard
I remember when we went to Mr. Jenkin's apple orchard. When we got there we used the apple pickers to pick apples. We also went into Mr. Jenkins' tree house. I love Mr. Jenkins.

by Paul

*A*t our Thanksgiving Day party, Paul was the only child who didn't have at least one of his grandparents present. And so Mr. Jenkins, a retired lawyer who became a teaching specialist in our school at the age of seventy, volunteered to be Paul's stand-in grandfather, Paul was overjoyed. Instead of having no one, he had someone Very Special. All day long he held Mr. Jenkins' hand or snuggled in his lap or made sure to touch him or be close to him.

At the end of the year, when Paul wrote his story for the Memory Book, it was a story about Mr. Jenkins. Although Paul chose to describe his visit to Mr. Jenkins' apple orchard, it seems clear that he was describing his entire relationship with this teacher.

Chapter

6
Being Sensitive
to Gender Differences

Photograph by Taro Yamasaki/Courtesy of Cranbrook Educational Community

GIRLS

In our opinion, there are definitely developmental and emotional differences between boys and girls. No one can say for sure, at this time, whether these differences are innate or culturally imprinted, or both. But the differences are there, and teachers should be sensitive to them because it isn't fair or wise to treat boys and girls as if they're exactly alike.

Since the overwhelming majority of elementary grade teachers are women, who identify easily with little girls, the needs of little girls in school are generally understood and treated with insight and sympathy. Nevertheless, there are some issues that even women teachers—or perhaps especially women teachers—tend to be unaware of:

Girls like to hug, to walk arm in arm, to hold the teacher's hand, to be close in a hundred little ways. This is usually endearing—except when they play with each other's hair and scratch each other's backs while a lesson is going on, or when they develop "crushes," which distract them from everything else! By and large, however, their need to touch and express affection is very sweet and will bring a frequent smile to your face. But there's danger that you'll indulge their sweetness at the expense of other needs that are often neglected: the need to be independent and adventurous, to offer an original opinion, to go out on a limb on occasion, to stand apart from the group and defend the worth of an idea that runs against the tide.

Girls also like to talk. A lot! This is a virtue that allows them to feel comfortable with language, whether spoken or written. However, they tend to talk almost exclusively about clothes, dolls, parties, and "crushes." Such talk has the charm and fun of gossip, but it also has the limitations of gossip. Your challenge, as a teacher, is to redirect their conversation—to get them talking about current events, books, and matters that go beyond the merely personal.

It will quicky become apparent to you that little girls have a strong need to please and do the "right" thing. This makes them good company and easy to teach. But it's a mixed blessing, for it means that they're repressing their anger and competitiveness, which then surface in undesirable ways. For example, girls tend to hold grudges, to pick on innocent but weak classmates, and to twist things a teacher says so that, when reported at home, the teacher's words are put in a false and unfavorable light. They do these things not because they're naturally devious but because they're nursing unexpressed resentments. Once you give them the green light to express their annoyance and competitive feelings openly, once you assure them that they don't have to be "nice" every second of the day, they'll become more relaxed and their behavior, although less "good," will be much better!

Finally, you have a responsibility to encourage young girls to dream of an infinite number of career choices and not limit themselves to the few roles chosen by the women in their family, school, and local neighborhood. Needless to say, this should not be done by preaching feminism but simply by enlarging their awareness, planting a little seed here and there, in the normal course of study and conversation. You'll be surprised how quickly these seeds come to flower!

For our poetry unit, each child was asked to select her favorite poem and memorize it. Sheila chose the poem "Girls Can Too!"

Weeks later, Sheila's mother told me the following story. Early one evening, Sheila's dad and brothers were talking about playing softball after dinner. Although Sheila loved softball, it was obvious that she wasn't included in their plans. The more they talked about "hitting the old apple" and "scooping up grounders," the more angry Sheila became.

Finally, she stood up and, with great conviction, recited her poem, "Girls Can Too!"

The men were stunned. They looked at each other, blushed, laughed—then invited Sheila—and her mom— to join the game!

BOYS

An inexperienced teacher may feel that boys are problems because they tend to be active, noisy, and less mature than girls. The truth, however, is that they're behaving in a perfectly normal way *for boys*.

In grades 1–2, many boys don't like paper-and-pencil activities. Their motor skills aren't well developed yet and writing is difficult for them, especially if the paper has narrow spaces between the lines. (Paper that's unlined or has wide spaces is a big help.) Boys in these grades prefer to play with large toys and build with blocks (and brazenly knock down what they've built) and, in general, do physical things.

Even while reading, they need to move around. When they're confined to a seat and desk for too long, they get wiggly. They need a carpeted reading corner where they can put their feet up or lie down on their stomachs or stand up and sit down whenever they feel like it. When teaching reading to these boys, you should inch your way, gradually, from level to level, using varied approaches. Variety and stimulating content are very important. Boys are bored by repetition and bland stories; they need to be stimulated or else their minds wander. They particularly enjoy the adventures of robots and monsters, and the sports pages of the daily newspaper.

Overall, in grades 1–2, boys will be more interested in playing than in learning about a subject. They can be coaxed to study, but their hearts aren't in it; they haven't ripened yet.

From grade 3 on, however, they'll become *passionately* interested in a subject that appeals to them, such as Space Flight, The Lore of Sailing Ships, Heroes of Greek Mythology (especially Odysseus), Heroes of American History (especially Lincoln), Heroes of Chivalry (especially King Arthur and the Knights of the Round Table), and perhaps most of all, incredibly complicated versions of Dungeons and Dragons. Boys of this age will explore their chosen subject with intensity, reading every book they can get their hands on, making intricate diagrams, charts, and models, investigating the subject from every angle and with intellectual thoroughness.

When a boy has found a subject that truly absorbs him, it's wise to give him a free hand. His reading will improve, his work habits will improve, and he'll discover the great secret of education— namely, that real learning is generated from within, not imposed by a teacher.

Despite their intellectual curiosity, young boys are not usually bookish types. On the contrary, they're very physical and chock full of emotions, which they express quite openly. Often they get very angry and start fighting. When this happens, stop the fight, but don't exaggerate the horror of it. They rarely hurt each other, they recover quickly, and they have no hard feelings. All is forgiven!

Boys will usually get rid of their excess energy on the athletic field. Sports are a marvelous outlet for them. Unfortunately, some boys are timid or uncoordinated and stay on the sidelines. It's easy to say "Well, that's their choice" or "Not everyone has to be an athlete." But if you say this, you'll be doing these boys a disservice. They really want to play, to be one of the guys, and to feel good about their physical skills. Try to get the physical education teacher to help out; if necessary, contact the parents and suggest after-school coaching. Athletics isn't the be-all and end-all, but it isn't unimportant, either.

Although all children should be taught to show consideration for others, boys should not be forced or pressured into doing things that they consider "girlish." In a recent magazine article, a mother with feminist values and two sons admitted, "I tried all those anti-sex-role things when they were little. I gave them dolls. I encouraged them to play house ... It never worked." Another mother, Anna Quindlen, was also forced to concede that reality was quite different from feminist theory. When her sons were born, she vowed no plastic guns, no Rambo, no G.I. Joe. She assumed this meant that her sons would never play with guns. "Wrong. What it meant was that deprivation would produce imag- ination. Guns from teaspoons. Guns from push toys held wrong end up. The ever-popular gun made from the index finger and the thumb. Even guns from Lego blocks." With resignation and wry humor she concludes, "I keep thinking that if I had a daughter and refused her a Barbie, she would learn to build one herself, which is no mean feat considering the engineering."

This doesn't prove, however, that boys are destined to play only with guns, or girls only with Barbies. A boy, for example, may sometimes *want* a teddy bear and at other times may go out of his way to express gentle affection.

At the age of seven, Alan was plagued by all kinds of fears and troubles. He needed emotional support, which he got from his parents, his therapist, and his teacher.

When he felt strong and happy again, he was very grateful to his teacher and figured out an ingenious way to express his loving feelings without appearing to be a "sissy."

After the class was dismissed at three o'clock, he'd find some excuse to return to the room.

"I forgot my homework . . ."

"I left my gloves in my locker . . ."

"I didn't take home the notice about the museum trip . . ."

Now that the teacher was alone, he'd run over to her and give her a great big hug and kiss. That accomplished, he'd run off, happy as a lark.

BOYS AND GIRLS TOGETHER

We don't want to give the impression that boys and girls are so different in their developmental and emotional needs that they have little in common. And although generalizations hold, they don't apply to every individual in every respect.

If boys and girls often like to go their separate ways in pursuing subjects of special interest or in playing sports, they also like to work and play together. Art projects, such as painting murals, sewing quilts, and weaving belts of straw appeal to them equally; so do team projects in social studies, such as a project on Life in

Alaska. Sports that they enjoy together are ice skating, sledding, kickball, soccer, and 4-square.

As classmates and playmates, boys and girls get along very well and enjoy each other's company. They learn from each other and about each other. In particular, they learn to get to know each other, not as exotic creatures defined solely by sex, but as individuals. Nevertheless, it's probably true that a young boy feels most comfortable with a girl who's a bit of a tomboy.

Alaska.

We wrote reports on Alaska. Mine was about Alaskan weapons. Ann made an Eskimo doll. I helped her put fur clothes on the doll. Ann and I had a fun time. Alaska is a good state.

David

While Eddie's mother was visiting Jacqueline's mother, Eddie and Jacqueline played together in her back yard.

It was fall and the game they made up was throwing chestnuts into a blueberry basket that had been nailed to a tree. They collected fifty chestnuts apiece, paced off a distance of ten yards from the tree, then began throwing. First, Eddie threw five chestnuts. Then Jacqueline threw five.

Eddie was pretty good. But, to his surprise, Jacqueline was pretty good, too. When the game was over, the score was even.

Vastly impressed, Eddie paid Jacqueline the supreme compliment: "Is it OK if I call you Jackie?"

Chapter
7
Motivation

Courtesy of Cranbrook Educational Community

INTERNAL MOTIVATION

Internal motivation is generated by the student himself and is characterized by curiosity and vitality. A self-motivated student, when he has completed an assigned task, expands the activity or finds a new problem to investigate.

As a teacher, one of your most important tasks is to distinguish between the child who gets distracted and the child whose intellectual curiosity leads him on to further investigation.

*B*rad was working on his drawing of a Brontosaurus. When he saw some other children measuring the room, he left his own drawing and ran over to see what they were doing. To him, everyone else's work always seemed more interesting; consequently he rarely completed any assignment.

Such a child, who is easily distracted, should be guided back to his own desk and his own work.

*P*eter was different. While working on a scale drawing of the dinosaur Diplodocus (estimated by scientists to have measured approximately 80 feet in length), he was told by a classmate, who was measuring the room, that "a Diplodocus is too big to fit in here." Peter was astounded. When he completed his drawing, he asked permission to measure the gymnasium to see if the Diplodocus could fit in there (supposing, that is, that it could get through the gym door!).

Such a child, whose mind leaps from one idea to the next, from a completed assignment to a self-motivated extension of that assignment, should be encouraged. Indeed, he should be cheered on!

Learning About Dinosaurs

I made a clay dinosaur and two cardboard dinosaurs. I had to write a report on a dinosaur. It was fun writing a report on a dinosaur. I made a graph picture of the dinosaurs. We made a dinosaur book. I learned that my favorite dinosaur, Protoceratops, is a plant eater. I learned what year each dinosaur lived in, too. I learned what armor they had. I learned where they lived. I learned how tall they were.

by, Dylan

Other children, shyer in nature, but equally capable of motivating themselves, will often do so when given extra responsibility.

*M*ary Ellen was a fifth-grader who'd volunteered to be a teacher's helper. She was fine at carrying out orders, but, although intelligent and observant, never had any suggestions of her own.

I decided to put her in charge of the computer center. Suddenly Mary Ellen came to life. At the end of the day, there was a message for me on a computer.

"Dear Mrs. C,

Don't forget that tomorrow is Timmy's birthday.

Love,
Mary Ellen"

The next afternoon, after she'd gone home, I ran over to her computer, curious to see if she'd left another message.

"Dear Mrs. C,

Class photographs are being taken on Thursday. Your class is scheduled for 10:15.

Love,
Mary Ellen"

On Friday she reminded me:

"Dear Mrs. C,

Change the calendar before you leave for the weekend. Remember, Monday will be the third day of the new month."

... and so on, every afternoon.

Once a child becomes a self-starter, she grows by leaps and bounds. Not only that, she serves as a model for other children, and as a catalyst who inspires self-motivated behavior in all sorts of ways.

EXTERNAL MOTIVATION

External motivation has to be planned and implemented by another person or group of people. Key motivators in a child's life are parents, relatives, teachers, coaches, neighbors, and television personalities. These people can stimulate learning through their example, friendship, support, and by raising expectations that are both challenging and realistic. They can also serve as important role models and have an influence that extends for life. Everyone has had an adult in her life who's made a difference: given her direction or inspired her with confidence and ambition.

In the classroom, external motivation must be carefully planned and controlled. It is essential that the teacher know each child, and work to discover the right key to motivate each child. To some degree, all children are motivated by recognition and rewards. A teacher can create positive feelings in a child by

helping him find his strengths, which in turn will nurture growth. (If a child can easily sound out words, instruct him in a phonetically based basal reading series to ensure the greatest success.)

praising and accepting the child. (If a beginning reader reads a sentence with expression and fluency, take time to tell him how well he read that part.)

praising the child through a telephone call or personal note to the parent. (For example, "Jon gave his oral report today and the class was attentive and responsive to his follow-up questions.")

displaying a child's work. (If a child is proud of a collection or project, prepare a place in the room for him to set it up for a few days.)

grading and marking. (Add a comment of positive evaluation to the grade, such as "I liked the way you wrote complete sentences in your essay.")

using stickers, stamps, and little drawings such as pumpkins or smiling faces.

A teacher can create positive feelings in the class by

giving everyone a chance to participate.

calling on children when she's confident they'll know the correct answer.

asking open-ended questions to solve problems, collect information, and make predictions. (For example, if you're about to introduce a science unit on turtles, you can ask the general question "What do you know about turtles?" The answers will probably range from, "I have a pet turtle at home" to "A turtle is a kind of fish" to "A turtle that lives on land is called a tortoise." The excitement of learning will come from pinning down the facts through research.)

The Stimulus of Experience

In addition to motivating the individual student, a teacher can motivate the group by basing classroom work on direct, personal experience.

W*hile teaching first grade, I read Sylvia Ashton Warner's book,* Teacher. *I was teaching in a school that was located on 300 acres of beautiful grounds. The inspiration of the book and the scenery led me to develop an experiential reading approach which would combine a variety of techniques for teaching beginning reading.*

Each week the class would experience an event. It might be a walk to the lake, science center, nature center, or art institute. Or the event might occur without planning, as it did one fall day when the class discovered baby turtles who'd hatched on the bank of the river by the playground.

The children wrote an exciting class story about these turtles, and so the reading book of the week had been written. The children rewrote the story to practice handwriting, used the vocabulary words as the weekly list for spelling and creative writing, discovered phonics patterns and rules, built word banks, and illustrated the story.

Each week the cycle was repeated, launched with a new event. The classroom library grew and the children's enthusiasm for reading grew with it.

A New Book

However, since children's needs and moods are always changing, teachers need to vary their techniques and materials to motivate their classes. A good new book is usually an excellent change of pace. Be on the alert for one that is topically or visually interesting. Save this book to introduce to the class when there's a lull in the day or when there's a need to energize the group or yourself.

*A*s I browsed in the children's section of our local bookstore, I came upon the newly published Journey to the Soviet Union by Samantha Smith (who was to die, tragically, in an airplane crash only three years later). The book had an attractive cover and beautiful photographs of Samantha, so I began to skim it.

I learned that in December, 1982, Samantha Smith, a ten-year-old girl from Maine, wrote a letter to the new leader of the Soviet Union, Yuri Andropov, to ask him why the Russian government didn't want to have peace with America.

After several letters and phone calls had been exchanged, Samantha was invited to visit the Soviet Union for two weeks.

Samantha's book is a written and photographic journal of her visit. Naturally, it doesn't examine the ideology of the Russian government or analyze the different proposals of East and West for preventing nuclear war. It's the experience of a ten-year-old girl.

Despite my skepticism about the Soviet Union's motivations, I had to admit that Samantha's book was fascinating to the children in my classes in the library.

After reading it to several groups ranging in age from seven through ten, I tried to figure out why they found it so intriguing. I concluded that they liked to hear about a child who had a strong conviction that was taken seriously by an adult.

They saw that it was possible to question an adult, even a foreign leader; that a child could make something happen, even be invited to visit a foreign country; and perhaps most exciting of all, that a ten-year-old could write an account of her experience that would be good enough to be published!

An Audio-Visual Medium

In addition to books—and sometimes in conjunction with them—plan to use other media: films, filmstrips, slides, tapes, and records.

On occasion, when you're reading a story, project the illustrations from the book onto a screen by means of an opaque projector. Or ask the class to illustrate the story and project their drawings while you read the story aloud. Or record a dramatic reading, using several voices, and play it on a cassette player while you show the pictures.

A Display

Plan to change displays often. When a child brings in a collection for display, limit the exhibit time by sending the collection home at the end of the week. Plan to coordinate bulletin boards and displays with curriculum themes. It takes a lot of time and thought to develop bulletin boards, but visual change is stimulating to the entire school. Whenever possible, use children's work.

(If you find that the sun has faded the background paper, it's been up too long!)

A Guest

Plan to invite interesting guests to the classroom to enrich the course of study. In the lower grades, it may be a parent or a community worker. In the upper grades, it may be a government official or a local artist.

A Special Day or a Special Event

Have a Pet Day. Invite parents to bring in the family dog, cat, gerbil, hamster, or snake. Schedule each visit 15 minutes apart. If the weather permits, do this outdoors, since some children are allergic to animals.

Now and then introduce a spontaneous change of routine—a party, a guest, a trip, a walk, a "Crazy Hat Day," a day when teachers switch classes, or an all-school project such as an outdoor "Fun Day" (bubble blowing, kite flying, outdoor painting). These days are usually scheduled in late spring, but it can be helpful to intersperse them throughout the year.

Plan exchanges with other classes and schools. It's exciting to have pen pals in another school, city, state, or country. If the pen pals are nearby, you may want to invite them over for lunch or a visit. They, in turn, are sure to return the invitation.

Schedule special events that the children can look forward to, such as birthday parties, holiday celebrations, plays, and performances. (It's best to schedule these occasions for the end of the day, although it's not always easy to live with the mounting excitement.)

Arrange special visits to the library. In addition to the scheduled library time, arrange for times when the children can go on their own to browse, read periodicals, or research a special project.

Plan field trips to supplement the curriculum, such as a trip to a science center or museum.

An All-School Project

January and February can be gloomy months in the north, because the festivities of the holidays are over, the novelty of the first snow is beginning to wear off, and spring is still very far away. This is a perfect time to add something special to the school program to perk up everyone's spirits. In our school we devote an entire week at this time of year to an intense study of one subject.

Planning, of course, begins months in advance. One person is chosen to head a small but dedicated committee that recruits speakers, coordinates the activities of different grades, and researches and arranges the trips. Several years ago we devoted this

Sculpture Week

When we had Sculpture Week we saw lots of film strips of sculptures. We studied about Calder and his art. The thing I liked the best was his circus. It was funny. The strong-man was the funniest, and I liked the lion tamer. He was funny also. Dylan bought two mobiles. Calder invented the mobile. A mobile is a sculpture that moves by air currents.

By Merrek

week to the study of sculpture, because most of the teachers and children knew very little about sculpture and we thought it would be fun for all of us to learn together.

Each grade studied one sculptor. The particular sculptors were chosen because of their appeal to an age level and the availability of their original work in our area. The second-graders studied Alexander Calder, who uses bright primary colors and whose mobiles and stabiles are well-defined and often have a comic quality. He also designs fanciful toys and, as a lover of the circus, designs clowns, acrobats, and animals. Perfect for young children!

The following is a brief description of what resources were available and what the week was like:

Film

Calder's Universe (25 min./color)
This film shows mobiles, stabiles, wire figures, and circus characters that reflect Calder's joyful perceptions. Commentary is provided by his wife, who reads from his writings.

Book

Calder's Circus (Dutton, New York, 1972)
This book contains illustrations accompanied by quotations from Calder, both of which reveal his feelings about the circus.

Trip

We went to the Flint Institute of Arts, which had an exhibit of Calder mobiles, stabiles, gouaches, and drawings from Michigan collections. The museum also showed a film of Calder moving his little circus characters and talking about them. It was wonderful!

Speakers

Several artists and critics were invited to the school assemblies. Some chose to give demonstrations; others spoke and showed slides.

Projects

As a culminating activity, each grade did an art project in the style of the artist it was studying. The projects were displayed in the hallways and all the grades took a walking tour to enjoy each other's work.

At the end of the week, we asked the children to answer the following questions: What is sculpture? What materials are used in creating sculpture? Who is your favorite sculptor? What is your favorite piece of sculpture? Why do artists create sculpture?

Everyone had a great week and learned a lot. Years later, children were still talking about "Sculpture Week."

TRADITIONAL AND PROGRESSIVE SCHOOLS

Generally speaking, education has two goals: to help children deal with the world and to help them discover the world within themselves. To reach the first goal, we require children to study academic subjects, behave in socially approved ways, and develop the skills to work cooperatively, meet deadlines, and perform well on tests. To reach the second goal, we urge them to become self-motivated, to work in their own style, at their own pace, and to measure success by their own standards.

Although "traditional" schools emphasize the first goal, and "progressive" schools the second, both goals are equally important. Children who can't deal with the world are misfits; children who lack confidence in their unique selves are leaves that blow with every wind; in a storm, they're lost. In your classroom, don't settle for one goal or the other; encompass both.

Chapter
8
Discipline

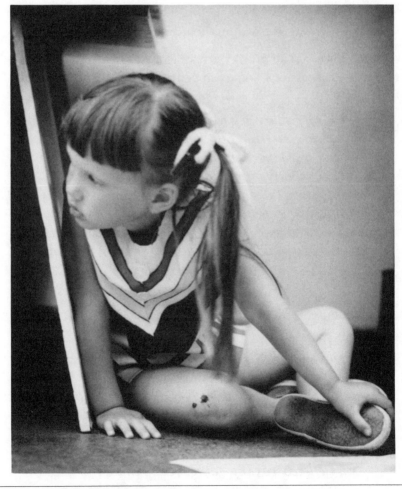

Photograph by Jack Kausch/Courtesy of Cranbrook Educational Community

WHEN YOU CAN SMILE

Be clear about your philosophy of discipline. (The school in which you're teaching may cause you to modify your style.)
To start with, we recommend that you

establish a tone of respect in your classroom so that everyone is expected to use good manners, practice self-control, and monitor his own behavior.

say no when necessary.

remove objects or playthings that are being misused.

use humor. Not all problems have to be addressed with lengthy discussions; some can be handled with a good laugh.

*P*hil came back to the lunch table with six Jello desserts, and put them all in front of his place. (Since meals were pre-paid, six desserts didn't cost any more than one.)
I could have talked to Phil about fairness or greediness or poor nutrition, but I didn't feel up to such a talk. Instead I smiled at him and said, "Thank you for being so considerate." Then I began distributing the desserts to all the children at the table.

Sometimes the laugh can be at the teacher's expense.

*M*r. Bell, the science teacher, was wearing very colorful plaid pants.
After he finished his lesson on the microscope, Julie raised her hand to ask a question.
"Yes, Julie, what is it you'd like to know?"
"Mr. Bell, where do you buy your pants?"

Naturally, you don't want to become the target of the children's humor all the time. When you find yourself feeling uncomfortable, call a halt. But usually a laugh, even at the teacher's expense, is a happy and welcome experience—and one that students treasure!

The Missed Spelling Test

Mrs. Robinson I remember when Mrs. Robinson forgot about the spelling test! We were practicing our play one day and she forgot all about it, but I didn't. I was watching the clock the whole time, and when we were done rehearsing the play, I went up to Mrs. Robinson and told her she forgot the spelling test, and then everyone started shouting and screaming. Then everyone went up to the room and got their homework and went home.

The End

By Kristen

WHEN THINGS ARE MORE SERIOUS

No matter how wise or saintly you are, there will always be children who are difficult, usually because they resort to one form or another of aggressive behavior.

Disciplining Individuals

Jimmy fights
He has a short fuse, is not articulate, and has been conditioned at home to be aggressive. To keep him from fighting, put him in structured activities that have a minimum of tension and competition. If a fight does break out, intervene immediately before anyone gets hurt; then help the opponents see the advantage of continuing the activity in a spirit of cooperation.

Jimmy was building a tower with blocks. Rob, who was next to him, was also building a tower. Jimmy felt that Rob was encroaching on his space and, in sudden anger, knocked Rob's tower down. Rob, quite understandably, knocked Jimmy's tower down. Jimmy exploded and began to fight.

I walked over, separated them, and asked what had happened. Letting each child have his say helped to cool off their anger. I then said, "Look, since both of you are working with blocks and there's only so much space available, why not work together to build a city?"

They agreed—children usually will—and the fight was quickly forgotten.

Kathy is a bully
Jimmy, who's strong, tries to dominate other children physically. Kathy, who's very bright, tries to dominate verbally.

*K*athy *was trying to force Joan to act in a play that Kathy was organizing. Joan really wanted to draw. But Kathy kept insisting that it would be more fun to do a play; she wouldn't take "no" for an answer.*

When I saw that Joan was weakening, in spite of herself, I decided to step in. I made it clear to Kathy that no one has the right to boss anyone else around.

Then I made it clear to Joan that no one should let herself be taken advantage of. "Stand your ground."

Then I took Kathy aside and reminded her that if she wants to have friends, she can't always have things her way; there has to be give and take; the feelings of others have to be respected.

Alex interrupts

He demands immediate attention for himself, even if it means disturbing the teacher, the class lesson, or other children at work. He is not nasty but is simply unaware. He has never been taught good manners.

*A*lex *was an interrupter. If other children were painting on the floor and Alex wanted to cross the room, he'd step over their painting, causing them to stop until he'd passed. If I was talking to a colleague, he'd break into our conversation without even an "Excuse me, please." If a group was discussing a story, he'd call out a question without bothering to raise his hand.*

But he wasn't willful. When criticized, he'd say he was sorry and promise not to do it again. But of course he did.

I decided to replace his bad habits with good habits. Each day for several weeks, I'd practice. I'd say, "Imagine I'm talking to Mrs. Robinson. You want my help with something. What do you do?"

"I wait until you're finished. Then I say, "Excuse me, please."

"Good! Now imagine that I'm teaching a lesson and I ask the class a question. You think you know the answer. What do you do?"

"I raise my hand. If you call on me, I answer; if you don't, I listen to the other child's answer."

"Good!"

It was slow going, but it worked. Eventually, Alex took pride in not interrupting.

Matt is overly active

He disrupts the class because he finds it difficult to concentrate for long periods of time. Thus he needs a frequent change of activity or one-to-one attention. (Often it's advisable to consult with the parents and the child's pediatrician.)

*M*att had solved the secret of perpetual motion: he was always getting up to sharpen his pencil, look at the computer, get a drink of water, sharpen his pencil again, take his shoes off, put his shoes on, get another drink of water, . . .

At first I tried to keep him near me, hoping that extra attention would calm him down; then I arranged for a parent to work with him in a corner of the room, while the rest of the class had the same lesson, meeting as a group.

When none of the usual strategies worked, I decided to call Matt's parents. We agreed to try behavior modification. Every time Matt managed to sit still for at least 15 minutes, I'd initial his Improvement Card and praise him for all the initials he'd earned. This helped considerably.

Further help came when Matt's pediatrician prescribed a change in diet, limiting his sweets. Eventually Matt's problem disappeared, partly because of the steps we'd taken, and partly because he became more mature as the year went on.

Nora teases

She tries to make other children feel uncomfortable, and usually doesn't stop until she provokes tears. This isn't an innocent prank; the intention is to hurt. Why? Because the teaser is angry. What about? Nine times out of ten, she's jealous. (If she weren't jealous, her anger would be more direct; teasing is anger that wears a mask.) The challenge you face is two-fold: first, to make Nora aware of her jealousy, and second, to help her deal with it reasonably and constructively.

Nora knows that Graham likes Jenny. So she whispers to Jenny, "Graham has a crush on you. That's why he volunteered to help you empty the wastebasket, and that's why he sent you a secret note yesterday asking you to go skating on Saturday, and that's why he did this, that, and the other thing. . . ." Nora continues in the same vein until Jenny blushes, gets flustered, starts crying, and runs to your desk to tell you the whole terrible story.

Knowing what you do about teasing, you take the girls aside and confront Nora.

"You were very mean to Jenny. I have to assume it's because you're angry at her."

"I'm not angry at her. I was just teasing her."

"Teasing that makes someone cry comes from anger. Are you jealous of her? Do *you* like Graham too?"

"No! I hate Graham!"

The rest of the conversation is predictable and ends with Nora in tears.

"That's all right," you say, comforting her. "We all get jealous on occasion. It's only human. But remember, if you make someone else uncomfortable, you're likely to wind up in the same boat yourself."

Ann tattles

She takes pleasure in telling on others to get them into trouble.

*A*nn came back from the girls' room and announced, in a loud voice, "Sandy and I were using the bathroom and Sandy stood on her toilet seat and looked over the divider to see what I was doing."

This kind of announcement puts the teacher in a bind. On the one hand, Sandy shouldn't have stood on the toilet seat and invaded Ann's privacy; on the other hand, Ann shouldn't have told on her friend in public. Since Ann is always telling on someone, it's hard to be sympathetic to her.

You have to talk to both children, letting Sandy know that what she did was wrong, and letting Ann know that she shouldn't make accusations in public—a quiet word to the teacher is enough.

Interestingly, of all things children do to each other, tattling is considered—by the children themselves—to be the worst. The reason, probably, is that children suspect that the tattletale is siding with the adult world instead of being loyal to other children. One thing is sure, if Ann keeps on tattling, she's not going to have any friends in the class, and she should be so advised.

Amos disobeys

He breaks rules, tests limits, talks back, and challenges the teacher's authority.

*I*t rained that morning. Before going to recess, I told the class, "You won't be able to swing on the tire today because there's a puddle under it and if you play with the tire, you'll get mud on your tennis shoes."

Amos spoke up, as I feared he would, "I can do it without getting mud on my tennis shoes."

Patient as ever, I replied, "That's a possibility, but we won't take any chances. The tire is off limits today."

However, we hadn't been in the playground five

minutes when I looked around and, lo and behold, there was Amos, swinging on the tire.

I immediately walked over to him and said, "Amos, I thought we agreed not to use the tire today."

"But Mrs. M., I don't have any mud on my tennis shoes. See?" And he stuck out his shoes—which of course were covered with mud.

I was tempted to point this fact out to him. But I didn't. Because I knew he'd say, "I can clean them."

Instead, I stuck to my original story and insisted that he get off the tire immediately.

"But . . . !"

I cut him short. "Amos, if you're not off that tire by the time I count to three, you're going to sit out recess for the rest of the week."

Reluctantly, he got off the tire and walked away, angry and sullen.

What had been going on here and why had I been so adamant? The disobeyer is a child who wants special privileges. He treats you as if you were his parent; and he seeks proof that you love him. He must learn, however, that you're *not* his parent, that you won't give him special privileges, and that if he wants your respect and cooperation, he's going to have to obey the rules.

Many teachers are thrown by such a child and give in to him because they desperately want to be liked, perhaps even loved, by each student. Remember, it's more important to be respected by a child than to be loved by him. Ironically, the surest way to win a child's love is to earn his respect; and he'll respect you if you teach him to grapple with reality, to learn limits. If you let him disobey you, you'll only teach him that immaturity pays.

Maria begs and whines

She seems to be asking but is really demanding. She's found that parents give in to this kind of manipulation. Like the child who disobeys, the child who begs and whines must learn that school isn't home and that rules won't be bent for her sake.

*W*e always had milk and cookies at 11:00 A.M. Invariably at ten to eleven, Maria would start begging, "Oh, please . . . please . . . please!"

"In ten minutes."

"But I'm hungry now. Oh, please!" (I could see her in the supermarket with her mother, making a fuss, causing an embarrassing scene, and finally getting her way.)

"Please . . . please!"

"I'm sorry, you'll have to wait, along with everyone else."

"But . . ."

"And please don't ask me again. It's very annoying."

Chris uses vulgar language

Chris curses to get recognition from his peers. Since cursing can become contagious, it must be handled firmly—if necessary, with a note or a phone call to parents.

*T*his problem will test your ability to keep a straight face. With great ingenuity, children will sneak in the forbidden words in a way that makes it impossible to call them to account. For example, Chris will run up to your desk and announce. "David just said 'Shit'!" Five minutes later, he'll run up and ask, "Is it all right to say 'Gosh'?" Most likely you'll smile and shrug and nod; then he'll add, "Is it all right to say 'Fuck'?"

It's hard not to laugh and admire his cleverness. But you have to learn to bite your lip and be stern. "I don't want to hear anyone use any vulgar word for any reason whatsoever!"

As we've seen, these aren't simple problems, so don't expect quick or perfect solutions. In some cases, be prepared to work with the child individually; in others, to call in the parents and, perhaps, the child's pediatrician. On occasion you may want to consult with a guidance counselor or school psychologist. For children with severe problems, you may even want to suggest an independent out-of-school psychological or diagnostic assessment.

Disciplining the Class

Occasionally the entire class presents a discipline problem.

I had a class once that was famous for its inability to listen. They never even looked up when an adult began to speak! When we were in a hallway, waiting for the next activity, they'd begin to poke each other or act silly.

I decided to use these times to work on developing their listening skills through dramatic activities. I chose pantomimes, songs, poems, and games designed especially for teaching this skill.

One game that was particularly effective was "Fussy But Not Strange." I told them that I knew a lady who was fussy but not strange. She liked beets, but not beans; pepper, but not salt; Molly, but not Susan.

"Why?" they asked, "What's wrong with her?"

"Nothing's wrong with her, she's just fussy about certain things."

"What else does she like?"

I pretended to think. "Let's see . . . she likes the moon, but not the sun; she likes yellow, but . . ."

"I know!" someone cried out. "She doesn't like purple—everything she likes has double letters!"

Waiting times can easily become trouble times. But if you're prepared, they can become an important part of your curriculum. There are any number of games and activities that children love and that can be made harder or simpler depending on the age range. Some fill-ins you might want to try:

Read off twelve names of states, cities, or famous people. Have the children put them in alphabetical order.

Ask the children to list all the people who work in an airport or a supermarket.

Pick a favorite restaurant, American or foreign. Then have the children list all the foods they can eat there.

Name all the things that float in water.

Give a number progression. Then have the children figure out the pattern.

Example: 4   16   256

Give another number progression and ask the children to continue it.

Example: 11   9   7   5   ___   ___   ___

At first, thinking of these fill-ins may seem like a chore, but after awhile it'll be a challenge to your ingenuity. Eventually the children will take over and do the job for you.

When a Child Says No

When a four-year-old says no, you can try to reason with him. Usually, he'll listen to you and cooperate, but not always. If you can't reason with him, don't be upset. There are other, simple strategies that are available. For example, if you want him to clean up and he says no, join him; company will turn work into play. Or if he takes someone's toy and won't return it, offer him a substitute. ("You *can't* have Ralph's teddy bear, but you can have this bear, which I keep in the closet for emergencies.")

However, when a ten-year-old says no, it's an entirely different matter. Ask her *why* she won't do as you ask. If she has a legitimate reason, respect it. If she doesn't, make it clear to her that you can say no, too. And that you will.

When to Look the Other Way

You may choose to ignore certain situations as long as they aren't harmful to the general discipline. Drawing attention to an event may even magnify it, whereas leaving it alone, under observation, can shorten its course. Children have predictable needs at different age levels. First-graders, for example, turn cartwheels everywhere; second-graders collect and trade baseball cards; third-graders write secret notes; fourth-graders play Dungeons and Dragons; and fifth-graders have an insatiable curiosity about sex.

O ur librarian pretended not to notice that the fifth-grade children seemed to be taking an extraordinary interest in poetry, gathering in front of the poetry section and reading intently. She smiled but made no comment. She knew that, behind the poetry books, the children had hidden books on sex education.

A Final Word on Discipline

As the year progresses and you establish a positive classroom environment and a personal relationship with each child, time spent on discipline will decrease. Eventually it will be minimal. Some problems will remain, however, and you should try to handle them within your own classroom. But if you feel that you need help, don't hesitate to ask advice from more experienced colleagues.

Chapter

9
Taking Care of Yourself

Courtesy of Cranbrook Educational Community

YOUR HEALTH

It's important to pace yourself on a daily, weekly, and monthly basis so that you won't become fatigued and susceptible to all the colds and flu that will be circulating among the children. Don't hesitate to send a sick child home. It's hard to stay away from her because she really needs you, and chances are—when you put that caring arm around her shoulder—you'll catch whatever she's got.

Set aside time for going out with your friends and doing things with your family. If you have children of your own, remember that they need special moments alone with you, and you need the pleasure of being with them.

Be sensitive to your own body. On those days when you have less stamina than usual, when your patience is thin and you're easily frustrated, revise your lesson plans and adjust the demands upon yourself.

Reserve your energies and ration them, because the school year is a long one. Be kind to yourself, and learn to accept the kindness of others.

Children are often very sensitive to their teacher's feelings and can be real friends in a time of need.

One morning, everything seemed to go wrong, and I thought it would be a miracle if I made it through the day! Rachel, my second-grade student, sensed this, came over, gave me a big hug, and said, "Tomorrow will be much better, you'll see!"

YOUR PHYSICAL COMFORT

Wear comfortable clothing. Dress appropriately for the activity of the day. On gray days, plan to wear something bright and cheerful. Wear comfortable shoes. (Remember, a change of shoes is a must.)

Make an effort to leave your personal problems at home so that they won't interfere with your classroom teaching.

When a child is driving you up the wall, remember that young children are bound to do that; it goes with the territory. Try to develop patience, tolerance, and a sense of humor. If you have a choice between screaming or laughing—laugh.

*A*dam was an extremely discombobulated six-year-old. It took him forever to get anywhere; he was late for almost every activity.

One winter day, he was late for recess. Mrs. Costa waited in the yard for ten minutes, then, her patience exhausted, went back into the building to get him.

She found him sitting on the floor near his locker with one boot on his foot and one boot in his hand.

She was about to scold him for being late again, but, controlling herself, she said, "Well, Adam, I'm waiting for an explanation."

He looked at the boot on his foot, and then at the boot in his hand, and then, totally confused, he asked her, "Mrs. Costa, am I going out or am I coming in?"

WHEN YOU'RE ABSENT

Inevitably, there'll be days when an illness or a personal emergency forces you to be absent. If you know in advance, inform the school secretary so that she can arrange for a substitute. Then leave the following materials on your desk: the school handbook, the class seating plan, your lesson plans, and a schedule of special classes that take place in other rooms.

If you don't know in advance about your absence, and have your lesson plans at home, call the school secretary, first thing in the morning, and dictate them to her over the phone. She can then give them to the substitute before school begins.

Finally, ask your teaching partner, who knows your children and their routine, to look in on your class to see whether the substitute has any questions.

Chapter

10
Relationships
with Parents

Photograph by Richard Hirneisen/Courtesy of Cranbrook Educational Community

FIRST CONTACTS

Your first contact with a parent may be an informal one that takes place long before the school Open House or the first parent-teacher conference. Often you bump into a parent unexpectedly in the hallway of the school, at a grocery store, a movie theater, or a school gathering.

Although these chance meetings can be very pleasant, they shouldn't be turned into conferences. Information given at such a time is likely to be distorted because you haven't thought about it carefully and don't have meaningful detail at your fingertips. So, even if you have positive comments to make, save them for a scheduled conference; in a social situation kind words tend to become inflated.

What *should* you say when you meet a parent informally? As little as possible—in the friendliest possible way. Something along the lines of "I'm really looking forward to working with you and Randy this year." The important thing—since first impressions can be lasting ones—is to let the parent know that you're an intelligent, caring person.

Open House

In many schools there's an Open House early in the school year, when teachers explain their program to parents. This is going to be a little difficult for you because, as a first-year teacher, you haven't been through a full-year program. To be safe, stick to the facts. Explain what the curriculum is in each subject area, not how you're planning to teach it.

Be sure to give the parents ample time to ask questions. Be honest in your responses. They'll know that you're a rookie, so assure them that what you lack in experience you'll make up for in enthusiasm, hard work, and a willingness to consider any suggestions.

Open House is a good time to discuss general matters that are relevant to all parents. After presenting the curriculum, you can make a pitch for parents to monitor TV viewing and to set a reasonable bedtime. Finally, you can suggest a number of ways that they can promote learning at home.

PARENTS AND TEACHERS AS A TEACHING TEAM

Some parents feel that as soon as their child enters first grade the responsibility for his education is now totally in the hands of the school. Not true! Educating a child is an ongoing, joint responsibility, and most often the child who blossoms in school is the one whose parents and teachers work as a team and together provide an environment where the child learns to love learning.

With a little planning, parents can reinforce formal schooling through games and activities outside school, when they're riding in the car, or preparing dinner, or paying a check in a restaurant.

In the Car

Review the weekly spelling assignment.

Read signs, addresses, and license plates.

Add "big" words to the child's vocabulary (not technical or esoteric terms, but commonly used words of several syllables—for example, "journalism." Children love to use big words; it makes them feel grown up.)

Read the speedometer and mileage gauge.

Make up math problems. (For example, if you're riding on the highway at a speed of 50 miles per hour, how long will it take you to get downtown, which is 25 miles away?)

In a Restaurant

Read the menu.

Have the child figure out the change you should get when you pay the check.

At Home: At Bedtime

Read aloud to the child.

Have the child read aloud to someone in the family.

At Home: Around the House

Label household items and furniture, where practical. (It will help young children, who are beginning readers, to expand their sight vocabulary.)

Practice telling time on clocks with hands and on digital clocks. (To make telling time fun, relate it to an anticipated event. For example, you can ask how many more minutes until *The Wizard of Oz* comes on.)

At Home: In the Kitchen

Read recipes

Measure ingredients

Plan a balanced diet

At Home: During Dinner

This can be a good time to teach manners. For example, the child can be taught to

set the table.

use a napkin.

use the proper utensils.

say "Please" when asking Dad to pass the salt or butter, and "Thank you" when he does.

be patient and not interrupt when someone else is talking.

At Home: Watching Television

Watching TV can be relaxing, a waste of time, or educational. To make it educational, turn the passive experience into an active one by asking questions that force the child to think ahead. You may ask, for example,

"What's Jack going to find when he opens the closet?"

"Will Ronnie take Dan's side or Teddy's side?"

WHEN AN EARLY CONFERENCE IS DESIRABLE

Sometimes an early conference can solve a problem that will otherwise fester and become serious. The problem may be poor academic work, unruly behavior, or an I-don't-care attitude. If you feel the need to arrange an early conference with parents, inform your supervisor. She may have helpful suggestions. More important, she'll know about the problem and, if your meeting doesn't go well—which can happen—she won't be taken by surprise when the parents call her.

*F*reddy was reading below grade level and significantly below the reading level of the class. I worked with him individually to find out if he had a lag in a specific skill area; then I studied the reports from his teachers in earlier grades and reviewed the results of his previous reading tests. After I'd gathered all this information and had discussed the problem with my supervisor, I set up an early conference with his parents.

I told them that, according to the information at my disposal, Freddy had been reading quite nicely at the end of last year, but was now having difficulties. He was reading word by word, concentrating on decoding each word rather than reading phrases and understanding the meaning of a story.

I admitted I was at a loss to explain his backsliding. I didn't think he had any emotional problems, as they weren't indicated in any previous reports or tests and, as we all knew, Freddy had been doing well just a few months ago.

Normally, at this point, I would have consulted last year's teacher. Unfortunately she was no longer at the school or in the area.

I asked Freddy's parents if they had any clue to this puzzle. Somewhat to my surprise, they seemed embarrassed. Finally, Mr. L. cleared his throat and said, "I think maybe it's our fault, not Freddy's. We were told to make sure he read every day during the summer, but we were so busy and he was having so much fun playing that we never got around to it." Then Mrs. L. added, blushing, "I'm afraid the same thing happened last year. After the summer layoff, he regressed. But I'm sure he'll catch up."

We decided to give Freddy a little more time and—not taking any chances—a little more help, too. In school, the reading specialist worked with him; at home his parents read with him every night for fifteen minutes.

At our first official conference several weeks later, I was relieved to be able to report that Freddy had made significant progress.

THE REGULAR PARENT-TEACHER CONFERENCE

The regular parent-teacher conferences are scheduled in the middle of each term, usually in November and March. The specific purpose of each conference is to give the parents a progress report on their child's academic and personal development. But the overall purpose is for parents and teachers to get to know each other.

Getting to know the parents means becoming aware of their values, interests, and temperaments so that you have a better idea of the influences at work on their child. It also means letting them tell you about his life at home, his relationships with siblings, and any family tensions (for example, illness, death, divorce, or the separation anxiety attending a mother's going back to work).

Having the parents get to know you means assuring them that their child is in good hands and that your judgment is sound and can be trusted.

Be Prepared

Well before the first conference is scheduled, you should be gathering materials in preparation for it. (The first week of school is not too early to begin.) Then, by conference time, you'll have a comparison-of-growth chart available. Effective preparation involves

saving samples of children's work—both classroom work and homework.

keeping records of tests, unit quizzes, and diagnostic tests.

writing down day-to-day observations, including anecdotes.

gathering information from specialists.

organizing all these materials so that they're conveniently at hand and you don't have to rummage about in panic during the conference.

listing questions for discussion in order of priority.

Encourage both parents to attend the conferences. If they're divorced, ask whether they want to meet together or separately

---

130

(first, check to see whether the school has a policy). If you're meeting with only one parent, make sure the other parent is given the same information soon afterward.

Remember that it's only natural to feel anxiety before meeting parents. Even after years of teaching, teachers feel apprehension before certain conferences. But if you spend extra time mentally preparing for a conference that you anticipate may be troublesome, you'll usually find that it goes smoothly. (Surprisingly, conferences that you expected to be routine may be a challenge!)

Setting the Stage: Outside Your Room

It's important to try to make parents feel as welcome as possible from the moment they approach the classroom. Comfortable, adult-size chairs placed outside the classroom door will give parents a place to wait if they arrive early and you aren't available.

To help parents fill their waiting time, let them look at children's projects such as dioramas, paintings, creative writing, and photographs of the children at work or on a field trip. Make sure that every child's work is represented.

Post a schedule of conference hours and stick to it. Remember that many parents may have allotted just so much time with you because of work commitments or a conference about another child in the family.

Setting the Stage: Inside Your Room

If possible, have the conference in your own classroom so that the parents can get a feeling for the child's daily environment. To make the parents feel at ease, set aside a pleasant area with adult-size chairs. Invite them to join you at a table that provides comfortable leg room and has sufficient space for all your materials. (Don't sit behind your desk. It keeps parents at a distance and, worse, may intimidate them.) If it seems appropriate, place a plant or bouquet of flowers on the table.

Conference Guidelines: Beginning, Middle, End

Plan the conference so that there's a beginning, a middle, and an end. The beginning should include a friendly hello and a simple question such as "Tell me what Betsy is like at home." It's not only information you're after—how she plays with her brother and neighborhood children—you also want to give Betsy's parents a chance to speak first and at length, to be in the position of telling *you* things before you begin telling *them* things. Remember, if you're nervous at the prospect of meeting them, they're nervous at the prospect of meeting you. They hope you'll tell them that Betsy is absolutely wonderful and doing magnificently, but they fear your report may be disappointing, even critical; and criticism—no matter how gently put—is hard to take. Most parents feel you're criticizing *them*. Inviting them to speak first conveys an important and reassuring message: that all of you are meeting together to *share* information and that you'll be talking *with* them, not *at* them.

During this opening phase of the meeting you should do a lot of listening. But now and then you may want to interject a comment or an anecdote that *supports* a point a parent is making. The best anecdote I ever came up with involved Don Banner and his pretty daughter, Alicia. Mrs. Banner was saying, with a smile, "Don spoils her something awful. I mean, he really dotes on her, makes her feel she's royalty." I laughed. "I know exactly what you mean." Then I told her about a recent incident in the library.

*T*he librarian had bought a beautiful new edition of the fairy tale The Princess and the Pea. *Wanting to introduce the book to first graders in a dramatic way, she put a pea under a very soft, quilted pillow, then announced that any child who sat on the pillow and could feel the pea was truly a princess.*

One little girl sat on the pillow, but admitted she couldn't feel the pea. Then another girl sat on the pillow, but she couldn't feel the pea, either. A third girl sat on the

*pillow with the same results. Then Alicia sat down with
great assurance. But after a moment she began to cry.
In a sympathetic voice, the librarian asked, "What is it,
sweetheart?" Between sobs, Alicia explained, "I can't feel
the pea, but I know I'm a princess because my daddy told
me so!"*

The middle of the conference should be devoted to your report
on the child's work and behavior in class. Since this is a potentially
huge subject and you have only a few minutes to cover it, you
should narrow your focus and touch, say, on three areas of concern. Doing more will accomplish less; if you give the parents a
mountain of information, they'll be overwhelmed and lose sight
of what's most important.

It's helpful to introduce your report with a brief outline: "Today
I'd like to review with you Kevin's math, reading, and some problems he's having with friendships." Inevitably, the parents will
interrupt you for one reason or another. If they ask a loaded or
provocative question, don't get defensive. Simply ask them to explain more fully what they mean, because behind their question
is an anxiety, and you should try to get to the bottom of it. If they
sidetrack the discussion to another topic, feel free to say "Let's
finish this point before we move on to that." If they want to discuss
school policy issues over which you have no jurisdiction, such as
lunch or dismissal, suggest that they make an appointment with a
supervisor. And if they ask a question to which you don't know the
answer, say so, and promise to find out and get back to them.

Chances are that any information you give that is neutral or
flattering will find a receptive audience, but anything that is critical
will meet with resistance. If you make ten positive comments and
one negative comment, you can be sure the parents will pick up
on the negative comment. Sometimes, to help them see how lop-
sided their reaction is, I tell them a well-known story about the
great acting team Alfred Lunt and Lynne Fontanne.

L unt and Fontanne made one movie, The
Guardsman. *On the night of the preview, Lunt was
in bed with the flu and Fontanne went to the
preview alone. When she came home, Lunt was*

*anxious to know how it had gone; in particular, he
wanted to know how he had photographed.*

*"Oh, Alfred, you looked splendid! Your eyes sparkled,
your smile was dazzling, your lips were perhaps a bit
thin, but overall, you looked tall, handsome,
distinguished . . ."*

Lunt sighed, "Thin lips, eh?"

The end of the conference should put things in perspective.
Remind parents that there's more to their child than thin lips and
review the plans and goals you've *all* agreed upon. Then thank
them for coming and assure them that you'll keep them fully informed: at mid-year you'll send them a final written evaluation.
Assure them further that if any serious problem arises, you're
always available for a special conference. If you run out of time
and there's obviously more to be said, schedule a follow-up conference for the next week.

After all the conferences are over, set aside a few hours during
the weekend to note pertinent information, general impressions,
and the decisions that were reached regarding plans and goals.
These notes will be a valuable record and will help to refresh your
memory for future reports and conferences.

MID-YEAR EVALUATION: WRITTEN REPORT

The type of mid-year report you send home to parents will
depend on the grade and the school. Many schools have simple
report cards that require you to give letter grades or place a check
in an appropriate box. Other schools have forms that require you
to write brief essays, evaluating the child's performance in each
subject and commenting on his general attitude, behavior, and
relations with classmates.

Whichever report you're asked to write, remember that an in-
terim report has two purposes: to note progress and to sound the
alert for problems.

RECOMMENDING A GROWTH YEAR

The January Conference

By late January, if you have a child in your class who is often unhappy and frustrated, who is still not doing well, and every day, in one way or another, shows signs of stress, it may be that he needs a *growth year* (a term now used to describe a second year in the same grade).

If this is the case, you'll want to discuss the matter thoroughly with your supervisor. If she agrees, call his parents to discuss his difficulties and to make clear to them that a growth year is not a judgment of failure but a prescription for future success.

The signs of stress that indicate that a growth year may be in order are unmistakable. The child wants to stay home from school; in school, he complains and cries, keeps close to adults, finds it hard to cope, and seems overwhelmed. He may say things like, "It's more fun to play with the kids in the first grade" or even— confronting the issue quite openly—"I want to stay in second grade again next year."

In addition to these signs, you have the corroboration of objective tests. The kind of test given depends on the age of the child. Younger children, 4–8 years old, may take the Gesell Developmental Test, which compares chronological age to developmental age. Older children may take the WISC-R, which compares ability to achievement. (These happen to be the tests we use in our school. Other tests, equally good, are also available.) You'll probably find that candidates for a growth year fall into four distinct categories:

1. The bright child who is socially immature

2. The late bloomer, whose developmental tests show an ability to do satisfactory work but who is performing below grade level

3. The square peg in the round hole: the child who doesn't feel at home with his classmates, his teachers, or the school

4. The academic struggler: the child who lags behind in many developmental areas, learns by rote, and isn't as intellectually capable as his classmates

All of these children can benefit from a growth year. The bright-but-immature child and the late bloomer merely need time and extra care to bring them up to par. The square peg and the academic struggler are more problematical. The square peg may be ill-matched with your school, whose philosophy and style are not suited to him. The academic struggler may be out of his depth and need a school with more lenient standards and fewer high-powered students. Nevertheless, it often happens that, during a growth year, the square peg wil' learn to fit in, and the academic struggler will learn to accept the fact that he isn't brilliant but can shine in other areas, such as sports, art, or music.

Begin the January conference by stating your concern about the unhappiness their child is experiencing in school. Ask the parents if he's equally unhappy at home. Invariably the answer is yes.

Next, go over the test results. Interpret them in a way that's easy for the parents to understand. Provide a frame of reference by comparing Warren's results to the results of the entire class.

Then tell the parents that you're considering a growth year for Warren, and ask them to consider it, too. Take a moment to remind them of the opportunities a growth year affords and to quiet their fear that it's an embarrassing proof of failure.

As the parents leave, stress again that you haven't made up your mind, that your attitude is "Let's wait and see what happens over the next three months." Advise them not to share this conversation with Warren. "It's premature. It can only upset him or make him give up." Then add, "I realize that this is new territory for you. Why don't you explore it a bit by reading David Elkind's book, *The Hurried Child*? or *Is Your Child in the Wrong Grade*? by Louise Bates Ames? They're both excellent and sympathetic. I'm sure you'll find them worth looking at."

The April Conference

Back in January, and even more recently in March (at your regular parent-teacher conference), you agreed to postpone a final decision until Warren had more time to "grow up," "find himself," "come into his own"—in short, to prove he had significantly changed.

Now in April, you can wait no longer. Go to your superior. Discuss your decision and the evidence it's based on—observation of behavior, classwork materials, test scores, and reports from specialists. If she agrees with your decision, arrange a final conference with Warren's parents.

When you tell them that you're recommending a growth year, don't be surprised if they're resistant, even at this late date. Usually they're worried about their child's self-image and the reaction of other children. Assure them that his new classmates (and his former ones, too) will be sensitized to their child's feelings and that no one will be left with the impression that Warren has "flunked." (At this point it's helpful to cite the names of several children who've repeated a year happily and to suggest that the parents of these children be contacted.)

If Warren's parents are worried that he'll be bored repeating a grade, give them some idea of how a teacher can individualize a program to make it more interesting. Instead of using the old workbooks, for example, she can offer their child new workbooks—on the same level, with the same concepts emphasized, but with entirely new questions and exercises.

Some parents may never accept your recommendation, and you may reluctantly accede to their judgment. But if the school decides that the child can't be permitted to go on to the next grade, the parents will have no alternative but to agree or to change schools. No matter what happens, remember that you're not the bad guy; you have the child's best interests at heart.

If the parents do agree to the growth year, they'll ask your advice about whether their child should have you or a different teacher next year. There are two ways of looking at this question. On the one hand, you'll know exactly where the child left off at the end of the year, will be familiar with his idiosyncracies, and will have already established a good relationship with him. On the other hand, a new personality, a fresh approach, and a change of environment can be very stimulating.

Each situation has to be considered carefully, weighing the pros and cons. Assure the parents that, if it's not you, the next year's teacher will be sympathetic to the child's needs and alert to any difficulties.

Because this meeting is so critical and reaches into the sensitive area of self-esteem, it should be handled with the utmost tact. It's a good idea to consider the personalities of the parents and, if necessary, to adjust your style to make them feel comfortable and receptive.

Preparing the Child

Ultimately, the parents have to assume responsibility for the growth-year decision and for making the child feel how right and necessary it is. If, however, the child is in the fourth or fifth grade, he should be involved in the decision. He may argue at first, but in a short while he'll come around and fully accept it. This isn't as unlikely as it sounds. He, more than anyone, will appreciate the need for it and will know about other children in the school for whom a "growth year" worked out very well.

If the child is younger, he can be told, rather than consulted. The best time to tell him is during the summer vacation. In order to take the burden of apparent failure off his shoulders, the parents can say, "We made a mistake by placing you in school too early."

No explanation, however, will completely cushion the shock. He'll need at least several weeks to work through his feelings, to express disappointment, sadness, anger, and eventually, relief.

A week or so before school begins, it's helpful to arrange an outing with one of the students in the child's new class, perhaps to go swimming or on a picnic. The point is to make certain there'll be a familiar face to welcome him on that difficult first day. This is also a time when parents and friends can offer support by focusing on the positive aspects of the coming year. ("Just think, the work will be much easier and you'll get good marks and you'll really enjoy school!")

*C*hildhood has a wonderfully selective memory. The trauma of the little boy becomes the taken-for-granted past of the adolescent.

At 14, Joel came across some photographs of himself as a third grader. In the most natural and casual manner, he asked, "Was this when I was in third grade the first time or the second time?"

Chapter

11
As the School Year
Draws to an End

Photograph by Taro Yamasaki/Courtesy of Cranbrook Educational Community

FINAL EVALUATION: WRITTEN REPORT

End-of-year reports become part of the student's permanent record. They are used as a source of information by his next teacher, and as a review by his parents and by the student himself. They're read very carefully and taken very seriously. Often, they're saved so that they can be compared with future reports. On occasion, they're even framed!

Each school or school system has its own style of report writing. Some forms include grades, others comments, and some are a combination of grades and comments. So before you begin writing your reports, reread previous reports that are kept in the permanent files, choosing ones from several grade levels. Find a model that's most compatible with your way of expressing yourself.

Inevitably, the prospect of writing all these end-of-year reports will seem monumental and, if you're normal, you'll find a hundred reasons to procrastinate. All of these reasons will be plausible but none of them will be true. To overcome your fears, set up a reasonable schedule and stick to it. Do one report a night, or three reports every other night, or ten reports over a weekend.

Do the complimentary reports first; they're easier. If you're writing comments, develop a general outline that can be used for each report. Fortunately, when you fill in this outline, you don't have to rely on memory. You can refer to the student's folder, where you've filed notes throughout the year. These notes should include:

Observations by you and other teachers who've worked with this child

Checklists of skills, such as phonics or multiplication tables

Progress in a sequential program, such as math or reading (number of levels completed)

Test scores: classroom and standardized

Samples of work

Write-ups of parent conferences

A good report should include an assessment of the student's work for the year, describing both strengths and weaknesses. Whenever possible, emphasize the student's progress. But don't skim over his weaknesses; they have to be acknowledged. It's a challenge to write about them in a way that will be helpful rather than critical (try to be an accurate reporter with a diplomatic style). If you can, give suggestions for dealing with certain problems.

If you've laid the groundwork during parent conferences, you might suggest summer tutoring. It's important that recommendations be part of the written record so that there can be follow-up by the child's new teacher next year.

If possible, type the reports (today's word processors are a great help). Proofread for typing errors and check for correct spelling and grammar. It's prudent to have your superior read some of your reports, especially ones you had difficulty writing or ones that are likely to elicit reactions from parents.

When you've handed in your reports for mailing, you'll be well rewarded with a sense of satisfaction. It's one of the few times in life that there's a feeling of closure.

GIVING THE CHILDREN A PEEK AT NEXT YEAR

Some children have an insatiable curiosity about what's going on all over the school. Their rabbit ears pick up everything! They find out what other children in other grades are doing by observing and overhearing conversations at recess, at lunch, while walking in the hallways, riding on the school bus, and waiting for performances and assemblies to begin. It may seem that they're preparing themselves to become gossip columnists, but in fact, they're preparing themselves for future experiences.

As early as the middle of the year, children start to anticipate what they'll experience in the next grade. As the school year draws to a close, they begin to talk more and more about next September.

This is a good time for you to capitalize on their excitement and plan activities that preview the coming year. Such plans might include eating lunch with the next grade or inviting the teacher from the next grade to read a story or teach a lesson to your class.

Often, children devise their own ways of getting ready for the big change. Some ask to visit older sisters or brothers in upper grades. Most ask millions of questions about what they can expect. A few manage to talk to the next year's teachers in the playground. (The more precocious child will already have "chosen" her teacher and will try to negotiate placement with that teacher, betting that flattery will ensure that the favored teacher will request her.)

You should encourage these initiatives. The more the children know about the future, the more they will look forward to it. By the end of June, each child should have one foot planted—securely—in September.

CLOSING UP THE ROOM

There are two schools of thought about "closing up the room" at the end of the year. Some educators prefer to have the children continue their work until the last day and leave the room intact. The children then go away with the memory of the room as it was all year long.

Other educators choose to involve the children in cleaning, discarding, repairing, and restoring. As the children sort materials, they often reminisce about the experiences they enjoyed or the projects they built. Sometimes they find discarded "treasures" and take them home as souvenirs. During this clean-up they can't avoid the realization that the year is ending—or the sadness of separation. But under your guidance, they can come to terms with these feelings.

We all experience sadness and separation in different ways. Some children are teary; others drift away, unable to say goodbye; still others show no feelings at all. But the hardest problem is the child who suddenly becomes very naughty, forcing you to become angry. After all, if you're mad at him, it means you don't really like him, so why should he feel sad about leaving you?

You'll need to be understanding at this time, even though you'll be exhausted and struggling with your own pain. Separation isn't easy at any age.

You must try to be especially sensitive to children who'll be spending another year in the same grade, changing schools, or moving out of state.

In general, your task is to acknowledge feelings of sadness but not dwell on them. Rather, accent pride in the accomplishments of the year, and pleasure at the prospect of a well-earned summer vacation.

My Teacher

The best part of this year was getting Mrs Robinson for my teacher. She let us do what we wanted when we finished our work. When we had our play she let me be in it I liked the play a lot. When it was time to go home after rehearsal one day she forgot the spelling test, and everybody cheered and yelled. I will miss her.

Mrs Robinson going away

me crying

By Adam

"Closing up the room" is so important because it's symbolic of all the endings and closures that are going on as the school year winds down.

THE MEMORY BOOK

As you can see from the selections interspersed between chapters, we've found it helpful, at this time of year, to have each child contribute to a Memory Book. The virtues of such a project are three-fold: it gives the children a chance to look back in a mood of quiet reflection, it provides a souvenir album of all their classmates, and it transforms the experience of the year into something tangible—they have a book to hold on to.

Chapter

12
The Summer After the
First School Year

Photograph by Taro Yamasaki / Courtesy of Cranbrook Educational Community

After the last child has hugged you goodbye, the last order form for next year has been filled out and handed in, the last meeting has been attended, and the last picture has been taken off the wall of your room, walk proudly out the front door of the school building with the knowledge that you've completed the year and, all things considered, you've done a pretty good job.

It may not have been perfect and you surely won't have fulfilled your ideal vision of yourself as a teacher, but you survived, and that's a real accomplishment! Now you deserve some rest and relaxation.

If you have a job for the summer or are going to summer school, give yourself at least a week before you start your new regimen. You need it, because the last few weeks of school have been a big push. If you can afford to take the summer off, do so without feeling guilty. Remember that when you invite your soul to loaf for two months, you're not wasting time.

Teaching is a profession that can easily become all-consuming and lead to early burn-out. There's no end to what has to be done. Therefore, you have to learn to set limits, to realize that, although you've become a full-time teacher, you haven't stopped being an adult whose interests, sympathies, and responsibilities extend beyond the classroom.

*Y*ou don't want to be like the mother of four young children who hadn't been with adults for a very long time. When she finally went to a dinner party, she suddenly realized, during the main course, that everyone was looking at her. Nervously, she turned to the man on her right and asked what she'd done. Pointing to his plate, he smiled and explained, "While we were talking, you cut my meat for me."

So, if you like to stay up late to read or watch old movies, go ahead! Sleep late in the morning! Take long walks and try to focus on thoughts that have nothing to do with school! Buy something new to wear! Play tennis!

Baby yourself, pamper yourself, and one morning you'll wake up refreshed, rarin' to go. And you'll be ready to think back over the year and evaluate yourself with a new objectivity.

EVALUATING YOUR TEACHING
MATERIALS AND METHODS

The Computer

On a rainy afternoon, go to school and work on the computer. Familiarize yourself with the programs the children are using. This time will be well spent and you'll feel much more secure in the fall.

Then browse through computer catalogues to select new software that will reinforce the skills you've been teaching. (Maybe some money will appear from an unknown source!)

Math

Take time to study the item analysis printout from the standardized test results. In math, you may discover that many of your students missed questions related to the metric system. If they're at the age when it's appropriate for them to know this, you might want to plan a more intensive unit on metrics for the coming year.

Try to use real-life situations. For example, cooking projects are always popular. If you can't find recipes in the metric system, convert measurements from the standard system to the metric system. This means extra work, but it also gives you an opportunity to teach conversion formulas.

Plan to add more hands-on activities to your program. You can never have enough of these! If a child is having difficulty under-

standing that division is the reverse of multiplication, use cuisinaire rods to prove an equation.

For example:

One yellow rod could be five units

One orange rod, ten units

Then two yellow rods would equal one orange rod
  $(2 \times 5 = 10)$

And one orange rod could be divided into two yellow rods
  $(10 \div 5 = 2)$

Reading

Read books by authors who are popular with the children in
your grade. Not only will these books give you new insight into
your students, but they'll provide a common frame of reference
for you and the class. Next year, in any discussion, you can always
make your explanation vivid and easy to grasp by referring to a
scene or a character from one of these books.

Experiment with a new way to motivate children to read. Perhaps you'll decide to use drama. Go to the library, take out several
anthologies of children's plays, read through them, choose a few
plays (on different reading levels) that you think will appeal to the
children in your grade, and make enough copies for each character. (The law permits you to do this as long as you don't invite an
audience.)

Plan to read the plays aloud to the class. Once the children are
familiar with the story and the characters, you can assign parts,
according to reading levels. Plan also to allow time for them to
rehearse. When they're ready, they can give little performances,
script in hand, for each other.

The best thing about using plays to motivate reading is that the
children have so much fun they don't think of it as a lesson. Indeed, some children may become so involved that they'll try their
hand at writing a play!

Supplementary Activities

Review supplementary activities suggested in manuals. You'll have more time to do this in the summer, and you'll feel great in September when you have new games for the children. For example: Make a bingo word game, substituting words for numbers, to help the child who needs to expand his basic sight vocabulary. You can use the vocabulary from the basal text or from a standard list, such as the Dolch or McCracken Vocabulary Lists.

Eliminate Inappropriate Materials

The fourth- and fifth-graders had very up-to-date paperback American College dictionaries. Each child had one! Wasn't that wonderful? It really wasn't. The print was so tiny that the students couldn't read it.

Since I thought it was sinful to throw all those books away, I contacted a teacher in the high school who was delighted to accept the gift of fifty dictionaries. Fortunately, the budget that year was able to support the purchase of new Intermediate Dictionaries for the fourth and fifth grades.

Repeat Your Successes

Remember the successes of your first year, such as the quilt that the entire class worked on, using their father's ties. This was not only fun for the children, but it gave the fathers a chance to get rid of ties that were outdated, over-large, or regretted mistakes from the day they were bought!

The Need to Change

If possible, spend a day with your teaching partner and brainstorm. Bounce ideas off each other and choose some new ones that you'd both like to try. Each summer be alert for the need to seek out change.

SOPHOMORE YEAR ON THE HORIZON

Before the First Week of Classes

After only one year in the classroom, you'll find that you feel like a seasoned teacher. Last year, before the first week of classes, you were scared. You were an outsider and, because you felt so

Our Tie Quilt Making

We all were making the quilt, and I was one of the people. We all brought some ties. Then we started to make it. Then we cut the ties and we pinned the ties together. We wrote our names and then we embroidered the names. Mrs. Tennant brought it to her home to put it together.

Rudy

alone, you were grateful if anyone sat next to you or included you in a conversation.

Now, on the first day back from vacation, you'll be sharing funny stories and summer experiences. It's a wonderful feeling to be back and to realize how much these people have come to mean to you.

The First Day

My best memory was the first day of school in second grade. We sat on the floor around Mrs. Tanner and she called on me lots of times. Then we told each other our names. And we told each other things about ourselves. I had the best time in school and it was great!

mrs. Tanner

me

Scooter

By Heidi

After the hellos, you'll hurry to your room and get busy right away. This year you won't have to spend so much time thinking about the set-up of your room and the organization of materials. This year you can focus on teaching from the very beginning.

You probably won't sleep the night before, but this time your sleeplessness will be caused by excitement, not fear. Once the morning light shines through your bedroom window, you'll begin counting the minutes until the children arrive.

Appendix

A
Learning Centers

Photograph by Taro Yamasaki/Courtesy of Cranbrook Educational Community

THE READING CENTER

The Reading Center can become an inviting corner in your classroom. With bookcases, milk cartons, or orange crates, you can define the center, and house reading games, instructional materials, and your class library.

For formal reading instruction, the children can move their chairs to the reading center. On other occasions, they can use the games for skill review, and the books as references for report writing or pleasure reading.

One school where I taught had SQUIRT once a week. The acronym SQUIRT stood for Super Quiet Uninterrupted Reading Time. Each Friday afternoon, for forty minutes, the entire school, including the custodian, secretaries and administrators, would take time out to read quietly. The children, of course, would snuggle in their reading corner.

It was a magical interlude.

The richness in quality and variety of books in the reading corner will help to attract the children. Each Reading Center should contain:

A variety of books on different reading levels (covering all the reading levels of the students in the class). It's thrilling for a child to pick up a book that he remembers was hard to read but now seems easy!

A variety of books for different interests: fiction, nonfiction, poetry, picture books (hard- and soft-covered)

Extra copies of basal readers (to be used for reinforcement, practice, and review)

Books created as a class effort, based on a trip or class experience, with contributions from all the children

Books written by individual students

Original books on loan from other classes (it's fun to exchange books with other grades)

Books on loan from the school library that are changed according to units or current interests. (At times you might want to emphasize one type of literature, such as fairy tales or myths.)

Magazines that are appropriate for the children's age and interests

Reading games, both commercial ones and student-made ones

THE AUDIO-VISUAL CENTER

The Audio or Listening Center provides an alternative learning experience for children and is an invaluable aid to the teacher. Once the children are properly instructed in the operation of the earphones, cassettes, and follow-along books, they can be self-sufficient, freeing the teacher for small-group instruction. (Don't hesitate to take time to instruct the children in the use and care of audio-visual equipment. It's educationally sound and important to teach children to care about the materials they use.)

The experience in this center can also be a springboard to stimulate and motivate the children toward other creative activities.

In my first-grade class, the children loved to listen to stories on tape. Then they'd go to the easel to paint their interpretations of the stories. As they became more confident readers and writers, they'd write different versions of the stories, and tape them. By the end of the year, some students even made slides to tell their stories, and trooped to other classrooms to show them!

You can inspire similar creativity by

changing the tapes and matching books at least once a week.

encouraging children to tape their own stories.

introducing the use of slides and projectors.

Most of the classic young children's picture books have been put on tape for individual listening and reading. In the Audio-Visual Center, each child can have his own book and headphone. As he listens, he follows the text and looks at the pictures. Some recommended titles are

Blueberries for Sal by Robert McCloskey

Caps for Sale by Esphyr Slobodkina

Make Way for Ducklings by Robert McCloskey

The Snowy Day by Ezra Jack Keats

For older children, the books on tape are accompanied by a filmstrip. Some recommended titles are

Bridge to Terabithia by Katherine Paterson

The Hundred Dresses by Eleanor Estes

Mr. Popper's Penguins by Richard and Florence Atwater

A Wrinkle in Time by Madeleine L'Engle

THE WRITING CENTER

The materials and equipment you'll need in the Writing Center are:

Table and chairs

Sharpened pencils

Paper (scrap and final-copy paper)

Materials for illustration such as crayons, markers, drawing paper, and glue

The aids needed for writing are:

Dictionaries

Thesauruses

Model strip of handwriting style

Examples of paragraphs and topic sentences

Story starters

Picture file

Prepare activity cards with ideas for writing projects. (To survive repeated handling, these cards should be laminated or covered with transparent contact paper.)

Children are very excited by language. In the Writing Center, encourage them to be inventive and to have fun with words. They may, for example, do some of the following activities.

Complete This Story

You wake up on Thursday morning, and you are invisible . . .

You find out that you can walk on the ceiling and walls . . .

You are growing smaller and smaller and smaller . . .

You find yourself in colonial times . . .

Answer This Question

What would it be like if there weren't any sound?

If you were a bird, where would you like to fly?

What would happen if everyone's name were the same?

Describe

A moment of disappointment

A pet

The smell of baking cookies

The smell of burning leaves

Use Homemade Books of Different Shapes

Turkeys

Hearts

Haunted houses

Recognizable silhouettes of famous people

Write in Secret Codes
You can introduce this by putting up a chart of the Morse Code.

There are many books available on devising codes, since this is a popular pastime among children. One book we like is *The Kid's Code and Cipher Book* by Nancy Garden.

Example: *I know <u>pirates</u> are seldom <u>sighted</u> hereabouts or <u>in</u> port, so <u>pursuit</u> in place <u>of</u> spying with <u>two</u> or three <u>small</u> boats or <u>rafts</u> such as <u>we</u> have, invites <u>attack</u>. We abandon <u>at</u> tomorrow's early <u>dawn</u> our search.*

by John Steere

Solution: *Pirates sighted in pursuit of two small rafts. We attack at dawn.*

(This may seem crazy, but kids love it!)

Write Poems
Have children read poems written by other children to show them what can be done and to stimulate their imaginations. You'll

find some excellent children's poems in *Journeys*, by Richard Lewis.

If, for example, the class is discussing the subject of "change," you can turn to Lewis's book and read the following poem, written by five-year-old Josh:

I know how daytime changes to nighttime.
Daytime melts.

Play with Rhymes

What is a happy father? (*A glad dad.*)

An excellent book for word games is: *Games for Reading: Playful Ways to Help Your Child Read*, by Peggy Kaye. She has a special section on rhyming games such as:

Invent Rhymed Couplets

I will pick a flower
and be back in one _____ .

This is a star,
It shines near and _____ .

Create a Rhyming Chain

First child says jump
Second child says bump
Third child says lump

and so on until they run out of words that rhyme with *jump*!

Learn Jump Rope Chants

Teddy bear, teddy bear, turn around.
Teddy bear, teddy bear, touch the ground.
Teddy bear, teddy bear, touch your shoe.
Teddy bear, teddy bear, I love you.
Teddy bear, teddy bear, turn off the light.
Teddy bear, teddy bear, say goodnight.

Play with Words

Make a word into a picture:

```
A NICE SLICE OF
 PIE   PIE   PIE
 PIE  PIE  PIE
  PIE   PIE
  PIE PIE
   P I E
    P
```

```
A NICE SLICE OF
 PIE   PIE   PIE
 PIE  PIE
  PIE
   PI        BBLE
    P    NI
```

```
A NICE SLICE
  OF PIE PIE
  PIE PIE P
   NIBBLE        CRUMBS
```

Complete This Sentence to Make It Funny:

I would recommend . . . a bath today.

Someday . . . you will learn to tie your shoelaces.

Funny Sentences

I remember making funny sentences. There were sentences on the board with blanks in them, and we wrote funny things to fill the blanks. After that we stood up and read our funniest sentences to the class. The class laughed as they heard each sentence. After school, we took them home to show our parents. It was the best assignment the class had ever had.

By Brian

THE MATH CENTER

The Math Center should be more spacious than the Reading, Writing, and Audio-Visual Centers. Young children need lots of room to build cities and imaginative structures and they need table and floor space so that projects can be kept up overnight or even longer.

Older children like to work in groups to do projects such as graphing and measuring. They also like to work with hands-on materials, and they often need time to expand their experience by working outside the classroom, where they can undertake an ambitious project such as designing a room with furnishings to scale or measuring the square yardage of the playground.

Materials should be introduced gradually, one at a time. After formal instruction—say, in the use of cuisinaire rods to build trains, towers, and mazes—the children should be encouraged to play freely with the materials. They're not merely playing, of course—they're exploring a variety of concepts, such as sorting, classifying, comparing, putting objects in order, approximating, patterning, sequencing, finding halves, and so on.

Finally, don't forget the obvious. To help support teaching concepts for young children, the Math Center should include:

Found Objects

For sorting and counting: shells, seeds, buttons, bottle caps, stones.

For weighing: beans, rice, sand, marbles.

For measuring: string, ribbons, yarn, milk containers, bottles.

For comparing: toothpicks, popsicle sticks, spatulas, tongue depressors.

Commercial Equipment

For measuring length: 12-inch ruler, yardstick, meter stick, tape measure, 6-foot measure (on a wall)

For measuring great distances: globe, maps

For measuring temperature: Fahrenheit thermometer, Celcius thermometer

For measuring time: calendar (with moveable days and numbers), clock (with moveable second and hour hands), watch, stopwatch, egg timer

For measuring liquids: milk containers (pints, quarts, gallons), cups

For calculating: abacus, adding machine, cash register, calculator

For weighing: scale, balance

Multi-purpose Materials

Cuisinaire rods, unifex cubes, trading chips, link numbers, play money, games (these can be stored in well-organized bins and kept on shelves)

And, of course, textbooks, workbooks, pictures, plain paper, colored paper, graph paper, felt pens, and crayons

THE COMPUTER CENTER

If you're lucky enough to have one or more computers in your own classroom or if you have the opportunity to purchase a computer to start a Computer Center of your own, take time to develop the center and the program.

In selecting hardware equipment, be sure the computer is compatible with the age of the students. The keyboard should be easy to read and finger, the monitor should be large and clear. For younger children, cassettes may be easier to handle than disks. Of course, price is usually a factor. Be wary of special offers—the company may be phasing out a model—which means that software will be very limited.

Research the software programs available for your needs and grade level. The availability of software and its cost may determine the kind of computer you get. Work out a system for storing the software—keep the system simple and the software within easy reach of the students.

Start out slowly, controlling the use of the computer in a way you feel is appropriate. At first, the students will take comfort from your help or from working with a partner. As their confidence grows, they'll become more adventurous, writing their own programs and solving programming errors by assisting each other. Eventually the roles of teacher and student may even be reversed!

*W**hen I introduced class 5A to computers, I soon realized—within minutes, actually—that Jonathan was way ahead of me and that I'd never catch up.*

So I did what prudent teachers have always done: I made him my assistant!

And, oh, what a help he was!

If my explanation was unclear, he clarified it; if my program was full of bugs, he got rid of them; if I wanted to extend a lesson, he brought a program from home.

The best advice I can give any teacher who's new to computers is this: Find a Jonathan!

Ways the Computer Can Be Used as a Teaching Tool

Reinforcement of Skills

To drill math facts

To drill phonics

To expand basic sight vocabulary

To improve reading readiness and perceptual activities

To improve reading speed

To do exercises in following directions

To do exercises in grammar

To do exercises in comprehension

Problem Solving

To practice critical thinking

To do simulations

Word Processing

To prepare rough drafts for theme and report writing

Programming

To develop the ability to write programs

THE ART CENTER

The Atmosphere

In the Art Center, a child should be able to experiment without being judged. The teacher should encourage him to care more about the process of making art and less about the final result. This means allowing enough time for starting over, trying a different approach, and using different colors. You can't put a 15-minute time limit on creative work and expect it to be satisfying. So, even though you have to follow a master schedule, make sure the child has the time he needs. If you can't extend the art period, be ingenious and find an extra hour later in the day.

The Area

Ideally, the Art Center should be located near a sink, where the floor surface can be cleaned easily when paint spills. The area should be spacious so that children can move about freely and, on occasion, do really big projects, such as a mural.

Storage Space

You'll need two kinds of storage space: one for art materials and another for work-in-progress. Provide open shelves for materials that are used daily, such as drawing paper, paints, markers, and crayons. Provide closet space for materials that are used less frequently, such as yarn, wallpaper, fabric scraps, string, wool, and styrofoam.

Provide drying racks for painting work that is in progress. Provide a large area, wherever convenient, for sculpture work that is in progress.

The MDR Formula for Art Projects

When you've planned a specific art project, double check that you have all the *Materials* needed.

Introduce a new project with a *Demonstration*. (Some children are timid at first and a demonstration gives them confidence and a guide to follow.)

Always *Review* directions for use of materials and clean-up.

Display

Which works should be displayed?

How should these choices be made?

What criteria should be applied?

These are questions that you and the children should discuss at length and resolve together. The only unbreakable rule is that *every* child should have *many* turns during the course of the year.

I observed a thoughtful teacher who knew how important it was to display, not merely a student's work, but his progress.
The class had been doing exercises in

perspective. When she selected Eddie's drawings for display, she selected three *of them.*

In the first sketch, Eddie had drawn one building; it looked flat.

In the second sketch he'd added another, smaller building to the background; it gave the scene depth.

In the third sketch, he'd added streets and trees; now the scene had scale.

No one had to say that Eddie was making progress. It was there for all to see.

Basic Art Materials:

Paints

Poster

Watercolors

Acrylics

Oils

Drawing Materials

Pencils (soft, medium, hard lead)

Felt pens of varying widths

Pastels

India ink

Colored inks

Papers

Drawing

Watercolor

Textured

Construction (variety of colors)

Newspaper

Metallic

Oaktag

Cardboard

Crepe paper

Fasteners

Scotch tape

Masking tape

White glue

Duco cement

Rubber cement

Paper clips

Brads

Staples

Fabrics

Alert parents and students to bring in any leftover scraps from sewing projects done at home (scraps that are brightly colored and have interesting patterns are best).

Scraps of Paper

Keep a box for leftover construction paper, wrapping paper, and foil. You never know when someone may need just a little bit of a certain color or textured paper.

Found Materials

This includes anything that has been discarded but can be recycled to create something new, such as boxes of different sizes and shapes, ribbons, and beads.

Equipment You Will Need

Disposable containers

Spill-proof containers

Brushes of varying sizes, paint mixers, and used toothbrushes

Easel

Drying rack or clothesline that can be strung across the area using clothespins to hold the paintings

Smocks

Scissors and cutting tools (be aware of safety precautions)

Tapes—masking, scotch, double-sided

Sewing equipment

Clean-Up Equipment

Broom and dustpan

Trash can

Sponges

Paper towels

Other Considerations

Plan group activities, such as painting a mural or sewing a quilt.

Plan for distribution of art projects.

Include names on all work.

Decide how often work will be taken home.

Think about practical questions such as whether scissors should be kept in a scissor rack or whether each child should keep a pair of scissors in his own desk; whether everyone should have his own smock or the children should share smocks; whether there should be a community clean-up or each child should be assigned a task.

THE PET CENTER

First of all, decide whether you want to have a pet. If you do, the location of the cage or tank should be far enough away from the children's desks so that the noise and activity of the pet doesn't disturb academic lessons. However, it should be near enough so that the pet becomes a part of the class.

Routines and responsibility for care of the pet are essential; without them, the pet will become an annoyance. Bear in mind the complications that may arise, such as insensitive handling of the animal and unwillingness to clean up. Prepare for illness, birth, death, and the care of the pet during school-year breaks, weekends, and summer vacations.

It would be wise not to add a pet to your classroom until you feel secure about most aspects of your program. When you're ready, you'll find that a pet adds a lovely feeling of sharing and caring, and offers a child an opportunity to learn to become a responsible person.

In one classroom they had a beautiful black-and-white rabbit named "Dolly." The children were forever watching her, cuddling her, and commenting on her characteristics.

"She wiggles her nose when she's excited."

"No, she wiggles her nose when it's cold."

"No, she wiggles her nose when she's smelling."

"Dolly follows the sun around the room."

"Her toenails grow very fast."

"She licks her paws and then rubs her face and ears to clean them just like a cat."

But the most popular question of all and the hardest to answer was "Why does he have the name "Dolly" if he's a boy?"

The answer to this question took quite a bit of research. After consulting many books, they found out that you can't determine the sex of a rabbit until he's a year old. "Dolly" was named when he was a baby and for some unknown reason everyone thought he was a girl. By the time he was a year old and they realized he was a boy, he already responded to the name "Dolly" and it was too late to rename him. Therefore, for eleven happy years, he's been "Dolly."

THE SCIENCE CENTER

Children have an innate curiosity about the world and get excited by everything they see, hear, or smell. Since the most effective learning happens when a child does his own investigating, the teacher's role is not to take charge but to provide stimuli, and be a source of information, if needed.

Materials to have available for spontaneous experimentation are:

Batteries

Bulbs

Thermometers

Magnets

Corks

Microscopes

Harmless chemicals

Wool and cotton

In addition, you can contribute books and displays of nature photographs.

But for the most part, let the Science Center be *the children's* center, filled with the treasures they collect—nuts, leaves, pine cones, bird nests, rocks—and the pets they bring in for a visit.

Although the Science Center is a special place in the room, science should be integrated into your everyday teaching. One

Bulbs in the Tower

One day in October our class planted bulbs. One day we brought them up to the tower where it was cool, and in four months we brought them in our classroom. We had graphs on our desk and every day we would mark our graphs. When we came in the morning we would measure our Daffy Dills with a ruler and we would mark our graph to see how much it grew. Our classroom looked like spring when it was winter outside.

amanda m.

way to insure that you include science on a daily basis is to schedule ongoing observation of the seasons. Some ongoing projects
might be:

Graphing the weather and temperature (Fahrenheit and
Celcius)

Painting or writing about the seasons ("Observations From My
Window")

Planting bulbs in September that you force-bloom in February

*I*t's wonderful to have a room full of blooming
daffodils when it's snowing outside.

B
Magazines Children Enjoy

Photograph by Taro Yamasaki/Courtesy of Cranbrook Educational Community

Boy's Life

Published monthly by the Boy Scouts of America, for ages 8–18; includes articles about sports, science, scouting events and other high-interest topics. What the boys in our school like best are the ads in the back of the magazine for such items as smoke rockets, krazy label stick-ons, hot pepper bubble gum, and such come-ons as "Make Money Fast: Grow Fishworms and Crickets."

Chickadee

Published monthly (except July and August), by the Young Naturalist Foundation, for ages 6–9. This science magazine for young children has a mixture of stories, articles, puzzles, and how-to-make projects. The step-by-step instructions are easy to follow, and lead to a satisfying product. The colorful format is especially pleasing to children.

Stone Soup

Published by the Children's Art Foundation five times a year—September, November, January, March, and May—for ages 8–11. It's a magazine written by children. Children submit original stories and art work and the publishers select the material to be printed. All children love to see their names and stories in print, and this magazine is one way to motivate them to write and do art work.

National Geographic World

Published monthly by the National Geographic Society, for ages 7–11. The stories are about wild animals, pets, hobbies, and real-life adventures. The articles are varied. For example, one issue featured "Amazing Ostriches," "Wheelchair Champ," "Animal

Talk," and "Satellites." Favorite sections are the supersize pullout pages, mazes, puzzles, games, and collector's cards.

Ranger Rick

Published monthly by the National Wildlife Foundation, for ages 7–11. The articles include information on human achievements and scientific events such as riding in a hot-air balloon. The fictitious character, Ranger Rick, becomes a good friend to many children.

Odyssey

Published monthly by Astro Media Corp., for ages 8–12. A young people's magazine of astronomy and outer space, it features information, diagrams, and photographs of the most recent space exploration. Sample articles are "How Big Are They?" (referring to the scale of the planets in relation to each other) and "Islands in Space" (all about galaxies). This magazine is fairly sophisticated and technical and would especially interest the student who is fascinated by planets, stars, and black holes.

Cobblestone

Published monthly by Cobblestone Publishing Inc., for ages 8–11. It's a history magazine featuring articles on events, places, and people. The following subjects were covered in recent issues.

Events	Places	People
Boston Massacre	Grand Canyon	Thomas Edison
Yukon Gold Rush	Mt. St. Helens	Helen Keller
Presidential Elections	American	Wright Brothers
Man's Voyage	Lighthouses	Susan Anthony
to the Moon		

Cricket

Published monthly by the Open Court Publishing Company, for ages 6–11. It's a literary magazine featuring short stories, poetry, and articles that are beautifully illustrated with black-and-white line drawings. Subjects range from "The Night the Monster Came" (a story about Bigfoot) to the "Valentine Maker" (a story about how "love notes" originated). There are always wonderful stories to read aloud to a group of children.

Other magazines you might want to examine:

Plays: The Drama Magazine for Young Children

Penny Power: Consumer Reports Publication for Young Children

Index